In His Arms

Angelic Signs of God's Love

A GUIDEPOSTS BOOK

Guideposts.
CARMEL, NEW YORK 10512
www.guidepostsbooks.com

ACKNOWLEDGMENTS

All material that originally appeared in *Daily Guideposts* is reprinted with permission. Copyright © 1980, 1982, 1983, 1984, 1985, 1986, 1987, 1988, 1990, 1991, 1992, 1993, 1994, 1995, 1996, 1997, 1998, 1999 and 2000 by Guideposts, Carmel, New York 10512. All rights reserved.

All Scripture quotations, unless otherwise noted, are taken from *The King James Version of the Bible*.

Scripture quotations marked (RSV) are taken from the *Revised Standard Version of the Bible*. Copyright © 1946, 1952, 1971 by Division of Christian Education of the National Council of Churches of Christ in the U.S.A. Used by permission.

Scripture quotations marked (TLB) are taken from *The Living Bible*. Copyright © 1971 by Tyndale House Publishers, Wheaton, IL 60187. All rights reserved.

Introduction was written by Marie Gangemi.

www.guidepostsbooks.com
Guideposts Book & Inspirational Media Division
Compiled and edited by Marie Gangemi
Jacket & interior design by José R. Fonfrias
Jacket photo copyright © Wood Sabold/International Stock
Typeset by Composition Technologies, Inc.
Printed in the United States of America

Contents

Contents

~ *Introduction* ~

IN HIS ARMS. WHAT A BEAUTIFUL IMAGE! So safe. So blessed. So loved. How we long to spend all our days there!

Too often it seems, life interferes and we do not feel God's loving embrace. At times it may even seem as if He has abandoned us. He has not. God and His love are all around us. Always. Sometimes we just have to work harder to see Him and feel His love. Sometimes we have to reach up and climb back into His arms. When we're tired and scared and discouraged and doubting and weak and all-too-human, however, it is very, very hard to climb. That's when God extends His hand to help us up or sends one of His messengers to show us the way.

Some of you are probably thinking that you are not among the lucky few who have heard God speak or been visited by one of His messengers. You are wrong. Too often we look for the wind, the earthquake or the fire, and do not hear the still, small voice (1 Kings 19:11–12). That voice can be heard clearly in more than one hundred stories and reflections that make up *In His Arms—Angelic Signs of God's Love*. In this faith-strengthening book, our Guideposts authors tell of their life-changing encounters with God and His messengers in ordinary, everyday settings. Their stories tell of hope and guidance, love and comfort, guardian angels (divine and earthly), faith, and the assurance of an eternal reward.

In His Arms is more than just a documentary account of visits from God's messengers. Through warm, personal storytelling, the contributors describe the impact and meaning of their encounters. They share what they have learned and remind us that God is always with us, that we, too, can experience His presence if we are attentive to the signs.

Some of the authors featured in this book have indeed seen or heard angels or received distinct messages from God. Others, however, explain how the beauty of God's creation brought them an enhanced appreciation of His nearness. An encouraging word or gesture at just the right moment, unexpected help in times of trouble, and unlikely "coincidences" provide still more signs of the hand of God at work.

John Sherrill comes to understand how angels are all around—whether we can see them or not—when he sees and later doesn't see the gems of color reflected in the evaporating dewdrops on his lawn during morning exercise.

An unfamiliar, experienced soldier helps recruits like James McDermott set up their tents on a freezing night and is never seen again.

Burdened with sadness, Mary Ruth Howes goes for a walk in a park where she sees a chipmunk drift off to sleep, embraced in the warmth of a late afternoon sun. As she quietly moves away, God reminds her that if His care can meet the needs even of this drowsy little animal, then how much more will it meet her own.

A billboard proclaiming the value of mud puddles helps Sue Monk Kidd regain her perspective and rescues her young son from disgrace.

In His Arms will also tell of miraculous recoveries from illness and deliverance from harm. You will witness God's tender mercy, as a young runaway is saved from the streets by playing an angel in a skid-row mission Christmas pageant.

Not all of the messengers fit our image of angels. Some of the angels look and sound a bit rough around the edges. Others are ordinary people like you and me, like the two couples who serve New Year's Eve coffee at a highway rest stop. God even uses animals—pets, strays and wild—to carry His messages.

Here, too, is the point of *In His Arms*. When we reach out to others, when we share God's love, when we witness to His infinite goodness, each of us is one of His messengers. Marion Bond West tells of a time when she was always rushed, yet always behind. God tells her that He put someone in her path who needed her, but she was too busy to see the sign. When at last she opens her heart to His intervention, she is blessed with His care, His assurance and His direction.

In His Arms also tells of divinely ordained pairings. A family that needs a hospital bed for their home comes into contact with a woman who has one to give away. A handmade gift restores a fragment of an elderly woman's memory. Even when these pairings seem to concern less-than-momentous issues—the boy who wants a hamster and the girl who needs a home for hers—they serve a divine purpose. This simple story, for example, contains multiple messages of love: mothers loving their children; children loving their pets; and the loving God Who can work out the details and teach a few lessons along the way.

The Evangelist Mark tells of two occasions when Jesus lifted children into His arms while He taught important lessons (Mark 9:36–37, 10:14–16). Even now the most eloquent of the angelic signs are often delivered by little children. As Brian Doyle realizes, his little son may very well "remember a place he was a mere four years ago." Children's innocence gives them a clarity of focus that life has worn down in adults. Their tiny voices may be just loud enough to carry God's most important messages of love.

The faith-affirming stories that comprise *In His Arms—Angelic Signs of God's Love* teach us to open our hearts and experience something greater than a mere tale can tell. They drive home the feelings of awe and wonder we can all enjoy, if we become aware of the signs. We can indeed rest in His arms! They are always wide open, ready to receive us.

"The earth is full of the goodness of the Lord," if we look with our hearts and listen with our souls (Psalm 33:5).

Symbols
of
Faith

≈

The Lord is my shepherd;
I shall not want.

—Psalm 23:1

I ONCE HAD A QUIET SPIRITUAL EXPERIENCE, unique to me, that might just be meaningful to you. I had come to a low point; I was trying to solve a problem that seemed to have no solution, and, though I prayed about it, I was full of fear and anxiety.

"Where are You, God," I asked, "You Who parted the Red Sea, saved Daniel from the lion's mouth? What about me; can there be a miracle for me, too?" And this time I actually listened for Him to speak. Usually I don't do that. I have so many things to tell Him that I'm not very good at listening. I closed my eyes.

I am speaking to you, He seemed to say to me. What I am in the process of doing for you is very fragile. Like a spider web. It is slow work, but I am creating something very beautiful, even though you don't see anything lovely just yet. If you move, or rush about in fear, you will surely run into the web and destroy all I am doing. Be very still.

I pictured the most exquisite web in the world, one spun just for me. Lights glistening on it. Perfect. God was not hurrying. And I was resting at last, trusting Him for the finished work.

In time that personal problem was resolved—beautifully.

—Marion Bond West

I HAVE ALWAYS LOVED THE STARS. When I was a child my daddy would come into our room on cold crisp nights, wrap my sister and me up in a quilt and carry us out under the clear sky. Then he would point out the constellations and tell us their stories.

My favorite was Orion, the mighty hunter with his three-star belt and his faithful dog. Even now I await his arrival each fall with the eagerness of childhood, and search for him in winter skies.

Last fall we moved fifteen hundred miles to an unfamiliar city. One evening I found myself unbearably homesick—so homesick I yearned not only for the city we had just left, but for all the homes I had ever known. As I stood on my back porch and poured out my loneliness to God, I suddenly saw my old friend Orion climbing over the horizon.

"Here I am!" he seemed to say. "Did you think you'd left me behind, too?

I've just come from those you love far to the east, and I go to those you love in the west. Does the world seem big to you tonight? I shall visit it all before dawn. Don't be afraid, little one. The God Who made you made me eons before, and He holds tomorrow in His hand."

Watching Orion's confident climb into the sky, I found my heart gently eased. Once more the whole earth was "home," the household and family of God.

—Patricia H. Sprinkle

*O*N A HOLIDAY WEEKEND I was frustrated and lonely, wishing for the love and care of faraway friends. Not knowing what else to do, I drove out to a tiny park several towns away from the crowded streets where I live. I was enjoying the azaleas and rhododendrons when I heard a rustling in a pile of last year's leaves. Turning quickly, I saw one leaf twitch, then another—and a chipmunk emerged, ears alert, nose sniffing for whatever delicacies might be hidden.

You're a beauty, I thought, *a lovely chipmunk*, all the while standing stock-still. He scuffled a few minutes but soon I noticed his activity slowing down. His head began to sink forward and his whole body became still. Only his eyes remained bright. I turned my eyes away so my gaze wouldn't disturb him, and when I looked back his were completely shut.

My shoe crunching on the gravel startled him awake and he began to scrabble in the leaves. But when I stayed motionless, he relaxed again in the pale warmth of the late afternoon sun. His eyes were drifting shut when he obviously decided to do the job right this time. He curled himself up into a ball, his nose under his front paws. He was safe, he was loved, he could sleep.

This time I moved silently, and left him to the last of his winter slumber.

If you can send your love to a chipmunk so that he can relax enough in your presence to go to sleep, a voice sounded in my mind, *how much more can I send My love to you—My love that always and completely surrounds you. Just open yourself to receive it. I love you.*

I drove back home, no longer lonely.

—Mary Ruth Howes

*I*N AN ATTEMPT TO "bring back the bluebird," my husband and I maintain fifty nesting boxes near our Lake Michigan cottage. This past summer we were delighted when a pair of these lovely, endearing birds settled into a box in our backyard.

Then one morning, shortly after five babies hatched, I found the male dead by the roadside, apparently struck while fluttering down for insects to feed his young. Heartsick, I picked up the small, limp, still-warm body. The loss of even one of these endangered birds is a tragedy. Surely this was a double tragedy, for the mother alone could never feed her hungry brood.

That evening the unbelievable happened. A pair of bluebirds from a nearby field and their five nearly grown fledglings appeared on the back fence. Daily from dawn till dusk they helped the widowed mother feed her nestlings. They stayed even after the babies were out of the box to assist in training them to become self-sufficient. At summer's end they migrated together.

Love thy neighbor? These gentle, unassuming birds *lived* their love—a lesson I badly need in this fast-paced age. And it's one lesson I want to practice every chance I get.

—Aletha Jane Lindstrom

"WHIRLY-GIGS" WE CALLED THEM as children. Those little single-winged seeds that come swirling down, hoping to find a spot of earth on which to grow, meanwhile covering walks and cars and porches with their golden clutter.

This morning our balcony was paved with them, glistening with last night's rain. The wooden floor was grimy from winter's neglect; it needed scrubbing anyway, and the storm had given us a hand with the water. My husband suggested we sweep the maple pods to the railing, then scoop them through.

The sun had come out and was beaming as we began. The blackened floor began to yield its dirt, the deep red paint began to show. But as we worked, more of the merry intruders came twisting down, as if trying to see what we were up to. Like children who always come running, getting in the way, eager to help!

As indeed they *were* helping, we both realized. These seedpods gathering under our brooms were the best scouring pads we could have. Each seed was pronged, sharp enough to pierce the soil. Each graceful wing was likewise tough and strong. They were a well-armed heavenly host descending!

Pausing to rest, we picked up a few to admire. What beautiful things! What artistry God uses to fashion even a simple seedpod. Each wing of palest gold was formed by tiny, featherlike fronds branching from the central stem. The little airship was propelled by the single wing, the nose tough and sharp, the compartment for its passenger delicately but strongly protected. Inside this sturdy cabin was its precious cargo—an elliptical seed of vivid green, soft as flesh to the fingers.

All this exquisite artistry and engineering, we marveled, flung into the air in such abundance to land on field or forest—or our balcony. Seeds ready to root and grow—so many that even the few that survive will richly replenish the earth for us!

—Marjorie Holmes

21

FOR OVER FOUR YEARS I searched for someone who taught Hebrew. There was a certain word that I wanted to learn more about. No one I met could help me with the word that I carried in my heart.

Just after my first husband Jerry went to be with the Lord as a result of a brain tumor, I crawled into bed at 4:00 A.M. Although I was terribly broken, I was also jubilant over his release from this life. He was free . . . healed. Lying in bed, I seemed to hear singing. Others in the house heard it too. In my dark bedroom, I listened to the magnificent-sounding words and believed them to be Hebrew, although I know nothing about Hebrew. I asked God what the singing meant. He seemed to say to me, "Jerry's home. This is a welcome home song." The words were so beautiful that I reached out and selected one, as one would a jewel, to carry with me always. The one I selected sounded like *"Sone-yah."*

Later I began to doubt that God had given me a word or that I had heard such beautiful singing. Then, while shopping one day, I struck up a conversation with the clerk—a young man just here from Jerusalem. We discussed our faiths. Since they were so different, I hesitated to ask him about the word. But something about his eyes was so kind that I blurted out, "Do you happen to know a Hebrew word that sounds like 'Sone-yah'?"

He looked at me for a few silent moments, then smiled. "Of course. But how can I explain the word to you properly?" he asked in hushed tones. My heart pounded with excitement. He chose his words carefully, "If Sone-yah were a flower it would be the fairest flower, the sweetest rose in the garden. The word is the absolute ultimate for . . . happiness."

—Marion Bond West

ONE THING I HAVE NEVER MASTERED is interpreting a road map. The blue lines and the red lines and the double lines and the numbers all mesh together to form a maze in which I become completely lost. My daughter summed it up well many years ago on one of our trips to New England when she told her father that if he entrusted me to guide us by the road map, we'd likely end up in California!

But, the other day I saw a sign giving explicit travel directions that even I could understand. It read:

"To get to heaven,

Turn right and go straight."

Now . . . just to be able to follow those directions!

—Drue Duke

*T*HE JOURNEY OF THE WISE MEN, led by a star . . . the glory of God shining in our nighttime sky. We remember this event each January, not because such epiphanies no longer occur, but to remind us that they do.

After the air raids on their city, Londoners were amazed in 1941 to find stately purple flowers blooming in the bombed-out blocks. The spectacular fireweed had not been seen there since Shakespeare's time. To the battered city they spoke of life triumphing over death. Where had they been for three hundred fifty years, these flowers seemingly springing out of nowhere? Right there, of course: a billion tiny seeds wedged in stone and brick, awaiting only the right conditions of sunlight and moisture to reveal their hidden beauty.

That's what Epiphany says to us: God's Kingdom is very near, awaiting only the moment of revelation. Sometimes, as in London, the moment is tragic and violent. Other times it's as quiet as a sunrise, joyful as a baby's birth. But always the moment of epiphany merely uncovers what was already there.

From the beginning, other nations were included in God's plan of redemption; the coming of the Wise Men was simply the moment when people grasped this. Epiphanies introduce nothing new. Epiphanies whisper, "Look again! God is closer than you think!"

—Elizabeth Sherrill

ONE NIGHT, ONE OF OUR CHURCH MEMBERS, Phoebe Greene, related some of her harrowing experiences of long ago when faith helped her to survive.

Born into one of Boston's privileged families early in this century, Phoebe married Ted Greene, a young Harvard medical student, and they went to war-torn China as missionaries. The Greenes lost their first child Ralph to meningitis when he was twelve years old. Retaining their faith in spite of their tragic loss, Phoebe, Ted and their ten-year-old daughter Joan kept moving just ahead of the invading Japanese armies, tending the sick.

Little by little, their material possessions were destroyed or lost, except some treasured print of the Madonna and Child. With everything else taken from her, these holy images became a symbol of hope and encouragement. At each temporary dwelling, she would unroll those cherished pictures and tack them carefully to the walls. They were her only beauty, her balance, a tangible touchstone of faith in that dangerous place.

Phoebe recounted the night when enemy soldiers came to their door. She and her daughter fled through a back door into the night, leaving the precious art behind.

This final loss left me breathless. "Oh, Phoebe," I blurted out, "I can't believe you lost your paintings!"

Phoebe answered as if her only thought was to comfort me. "But, my dear, you see, we still had the stars."

The stars.... Of course, Phoebe by now had seen beyond worldly attachments. God could be found wherever one looked, and for Phoebe He was found by looking up.

Phoebe Greene's words still sing in my mind. To be like Phoebe, I would have to keep believing in people, even when they disappoint me. I would have to keep loving people, even when they didn't seem to love me. I would have to keep forgiving people, even when they refused to forgive me. And I would have to keep trusting God, no matter what trouble unfolded before me. But, you know, perhaps that's not an impossible task ... if I look up and focus on one of Phoebe's stars.

—Pam Kidd

MY BROTHER OLIVER WAS BLIND, mute, crippled and severely retarded. He lived in our home in a corner of a room with yellow walls, under a window, for his entire life. Each bit of food he ate was brought to his lips by another human being.

One afternoon we were playing in the yard, my brothers and sisters and I, when a friend from school joined us. After an hour of playing ball, Maria, my younger sister who was nine at the time, said to our friend, "You want to see an angel? We got one."

Our schoolmate was curious and skeptical. "Yeah, where?"

Maria led our friend into the house and into Oliver's room. "There. There is our angel."

I do not know what our school friend thought, but I know now, thirty years later, that my sister was right. Oliver was an angel. He was born in

April. He never committed a sin. He never grew. He never learned how to speak. Oliver was a baby for thirty-two years. My mother always said, "Christopher, when you go to Heaven, Oliver will be the first person there to greet you. He will run and dance and laugh."

If you place your hands upon your eyes, if you place your hands upon your lips, if you place your hand upon your beating heart, you will recognize the child that is still in you. The child in you has not died, but has changed. That is the change we are promised after death.

If you visit the Benedictine Monastery in Weston, Vermont, please visit the grave of Oliver, my brother, and place spring flowers upon his grave.

—Christopher de Vinck

*T*HE LIGHTS WERE DIM and the hospital wing was very quiet. In Room 322, a minister lay dying. Softly, there came the sound of someone singing:

"No one ever cared for me like Jesus . . .
Oh, how He cares for me."

The pastor opened his eyes and saw a hospital janitor mopping the floor just outside his door. As the janitor sang on, the pastor began to nod, slowly, just enough to cause the janitor to see the movement and come to his bedside.

The janitor reached for the pastor's hands, took them in his own, and prayed aloud, "Lord, put new strength in this man." Then he went on about his mopping.

From that moment on, the minister began to recover. Today he's pastoring again.

This actually happened. I think of it often, for it reminds me again and again that all of us can be ministers.

—Marion Bond West

*S*OMEWHERE IN THE CLUTTER of mail that came the other day—bills and catalogues and so on—was a reproduction of a drawing called *The Joyful Christ* by an artist named R.S. Riddick. Just a pen-and-ink sketch of the head and shoulders of a bearded young man, smiling at something or somebody off to the viewer's right, smiling with such warmth and spontaneity that I pinned it up over my desk so that I see it when I look up.

Whenever I do, I find myself wondering: *What is He smiling about?* Is He encouraging some shy little street urchin to sit on His lap? Is He gently urging Martha not to be such a fussbudget? Has He just told the disciples that it is easier for a camel to go through the eye of a needle than for a rich man to enter the kingdom of God, and are all of them laughing because they know, as Bible scholars tell us, that the "eye of the needle" was the name for a small gate in the city wall of Jerusalem where a loaded camel had to struggle to get through?

Or, perhaps, is He saying to me, "Come now, don't fret so much about the future and what it may or may not hold. Sure, you have some problems. Everyone does. But you also have built into you by your Heavenly Father the resources to cope with them. Besides, I am right here beside you, and if I can smile at your fears, what are you so worried about?"

A "Joyful Christ"? That's one thing He surely was. That's one thing He wants us to remember about Him today.

—Arthur Gordon

ONE RED-AND-GOLD AUTUMN DAY my six-year-old son's spaniel, Captain Marvel, got sick. The vet said it was a severe infection and administered a shot. But Captain Marvel only got worse. For two days he whimpered in his doghouse, refused food and water and couldn't get up. My son hovered over him like a sad little cloud. I was sure the poor dog was dying, so . . . back to the vet. This time he offered to put the dog to sleep. I refused. No, Captain Marvel would die in his own bed.

I broke the news to Bob gently. He ran to the doghouse, fell in a pile of shriveled leaves and prayed this simple prayer: "God, please make Captain well." Then he rubbed Captain's ears. "You'll be fine," he told the dog. But I felt nervous. Now how would I explain the dog's death?

Early the next morning as I shuffled past the patio glass, I saw a streak of brown-and-white fur flash across the yard. There was the dog racing for his feeding bowl as though in a dog-food commercial. Captain Marvel was alive, well and hungry.

Was it those few seconds between a trusting little boy and a tender-hearted Father that had made the difference? Was it a child's simple trust? Perhaps I'll never know the answer. But how I yearn to find my own child-like faith again.

—Sue Monk Kidd

*A*WESOME!" "*RADICAL!*" "*OH, WOW!*" It is ten o'clock at night and my family is standing in the middle of a frozen lake in pajamas and coats, if you can believe it. We're staring at the *aurora borealis*—the northern lights—flickering and flashing, cascading and dancing across the black-velvet sky. There is a curtain of green, a sunburst of yellow, a ribbon of pink. "Glory to God," I speak into the night.

Eskimos believed that the aurora was alive and if you whistled at it, it would come closer out of curiosity. Actually, the aurora is a gigantic electrical phenomenon, a series of flashes that occur simultaneously at the North and South Poles, discharging more electric power in one evening than the entire United States consumes in a year! Its origins are in the solar winds: high-speed, charged particles streaming out from the sun. When the solar wind's magnetic field intersects with the Earth's magnetic field—strongest at the poles—we see the aurora.

It's amazing how our universe is both mysterious and explainable all in one. I see God like that, too. Some days I understand Him clearly and say with confidence, "I know Whom I have believed." Other days I cannot begin to comprehend His ways, and I fall back in awe before His mysteries.

Aren't both perspectives important to believing? What I understand by faith causes me to trust God. But, oh, let there be glorious mysteries, too! They hold me spellbound, like northern lights flashing in the night sky.

—Carol Knapp

WHEN I LIVED ON THE EAST COAST of South Carolina, I fell in love with dolphins. I always smiled when I saw them arching and diving in the ocean. But my first encounter with these playful creatures was not so pleasant. One day, while swimming in the ocean, I looked up to see a fin cutting through the water not twenty feet from me. Thinking that I was soon to be dinner for a shark, I froze. My companion, an accomplished surfer, looked at my horrified face, then at the fin, and burst into laughter. I had not yet learned to recognize the distinctive difference between a shark's triangular fin and a dolphin's rounded one. Some lessons, once learned, are never forgotten!

Somewhere along the way, the dolphin also became a meaningful symbol of God for me. Every time I walk on the beach, I want to see a dolphin. But dolphins don't appear on command. When I do see one, it's often a fleeting glimpse: a gleaming gray back breaking the surface; the trace of a fin above a wave; or just the distinct wheezing sound of a dolphin breathing through its blowhole. Whenever I see a dolphin, I feel that I've received a gift.

Late this afternoon, I saw a blazing Texas sun dipping toward the vast horizon, silhouetting an arid land in dark, muted beauty. For an instant I felt the tingle of God's presence. Then the sun dropped behind the hillside and I was left with a residue of joy.

God is never on the surface for very long. Although He is always with me, His ways are often hidden; His face cannot be seen. But I am thankful for those precious fleeting glimpses of His wonder.

—Scott Walker

*J*ENNY IS AN UNPREPOSSESSING CHILD. Shy, awkward, a little ungainly, she seemed an unlikely choice for Mary in the church Christmas pageant. No parent was heard to complain, but then our pageant has always had its casting irregularities (including the boy who insisted on playing a camel one year).

That morning, there was the usual display of nerves and high spirits, the flashing of cameras, the last-minute tweaking of a halo, the mouthing of a well-rehearsed line. I went to my spot in the gallery to watch. The Annunciation came early. A teenaged boy wearing sneakers underneath his white robe told Mary that she would bear the Baby Jesus. Jenny, dressed in blue, walked down the center aisle and responded, "My soul doth magnify the Lord, and my spirit hath rejoiced in God my Saviour" (Luke 1:46–47).

Jenny's voice was strong and confident, filling the church. Her diction was crystal clear. To my amazement and to everyone else's, she went on, "For he hath regarded the low estate of his handmaiden" (Luke 1:46–55). She was going to recite all ten verses of Luke's song of Mary. We sat on the edge of our pews. Before our eyes, Jenny was transformed from a nine-year-old wallflower to a brave, commanding soul.

Never missing a beat, she made her way through the entire speech. When she was finished, the congregation burst into spontaneous applause. Better than any preacher, Jenny had given us the message of that moment. God could take a young peasant girl and make her the mother of His Son. God could transform a life into something awe-inspiring.

—Rick Hamlin

I COULD HARDLY BELIEVE IT. A flower, a single bloom of impatiens, pure white, no more than three inches high, growing on the street in front of my apartment house. I came upon it when Shep and I returned from our morning walk. We stopped in amazement. There it was, hugging the curbside, with no noticeable reason for its being, no birthing dirt, just cement and stone. And what an unlikely spot for it, since the corner of Eighty-first Street and Central Park West is inordinately busy, with traffic emerging from the park and buses rolling up to their appointed stop.

"Carlos," I cried out to our doorman, "look at this!" He came and was just as excited as I was.

"It's unbelievable," he said, shaking his head. "Beautiful."

We chatted awhile, trying to figure what we should do to protect it, and just then a crosstown M79 bus rolled up, its wheels ending our dilemma.

What minuscule womb that I could not see lay hidden in the pavement? What seed could find its way there? What courage it took to struggle up to birth, and then what matchless beauty that was so fleeting.

I went into the building knowing I had received a Godsend.

—Van Varner

I COLLECT ANGELS BECAUSE I BELIEVE ANGELS are real. I never put away my Christmas angels. My smallest angel could stand on my thumbnail, and the largest one is over two feet high. Some sit, some stand, one lies on his tummy. We have angels on the wall over our bed, and other angels appear to watch us eat from their kitchen window perch. One calico angel was handmade by Callie Cobb, a woman in her nineties. And outside in a small garden there is an angel with hands clasped, as though praying.

A year ago I bought a heavy concrete angel about twenty inches tall to sit on top of our brick-encased mailbox. One morning the new angel was gone. My husband Gene went to the police and filled out a "missing angel" report.

When I talked to God about this lost angel, I got the distinct impression that He said, *Take heart, I'm sending you another.* Four days later, in the mail, I received a carefully wrapped package. Inside was a four-inch, elegant, perfectly carved Fontanini angel. The note from the anonymous giver said, "Somehow this angel seemed to have your name on it."

—Marion Bond West

*T*HE WONDER OF GOD'S LOVE, my husband George and I discovered, is often found at rest stops, those small green islands so clean and quiet after the roar of the highway. You meet so many nice people in that brief pause en route to your destination, people who become instant friends, stopping to admire your dogs, happy to share a map or their field glasses, or even to help you if you have car trouble.

And during holiday weekends, at most of these stops there is someone on duty to provide free coffee. One night as we came out of the building, we noticed the sign FREE COFFEE and a converted trailer where a few people were gathered. Although neither of us really wanted coffee, we decided, "Let's have some!" And there at the big open caravan, we found two middle-aged couples beaming behind a steaming urn.

"Who sponsors you?" I asked the pretty, gray-haired woman who handed me the cup.

"*Us!*" grinned her husband. "The four of us"—he introduced himself and his companions—"have been here every year for fifteen years and have never had more fun."

"What a nice, hospitable thing to do," I said.

"Well, actually it's more than that. It's to try to slow people down, and especially if they've been drinking, help sober them up." We all gathered closer to discuss the terrible toll of people killed on our highways during the holidays, and how good it feels to know you may have saved even a few by this simple, friendly act.

"We really enjoy doing it," they said. "It helps our marriages. We're closer as couples. And we meet so many wonderful people—like you!

—Marjorie Holmes

*D*URING HER ENTIRE LIFE, our springer spaniel Sushi slept under my husband Keith's side of the bed, but the night before her final appointment at the vet—after months of fighting liver disease—she climbed onto the bed on my side and slept beside me, her head on my pillow. I was certain she knew the next morning would be her last.

Keith and I were holding her at the vet's office when she received the injection and quietly ceased breathing. Blinded with tears, I went back to the front office to pay; Keith followed, also grieving, but holding back his tears until no one but I could see. As I stood at the counter, fumbling for my checkbook, I felt a light touch on my arm and looked over to see an elderly Japanese-American woman beside me.

"Did you just put your dog down?" she asked.

I nodded, not able to speak yet. She indicated the other side of the room where an elderly, stoical Japanese-American man sat holding the leash of a white-faced Irish setter. "We, too," she said, her eyes glistening. Suddenly, she and I were hugging each other, crying openly, while our men watched us, unmoving.

I never knew who she was, and I never saw her again. She was the sharing of grief I needed, at the moment I needed it, a stranger who carried comfort with her and sought it from me. I think God gives us moments like these, the gift of strangers who exactly mirror us, who touch us for a precious second and then move on, so that we will always remember we are not alone.

—Rhoda Blecker

One Sunday morning, while visiting a friend's church, I was intrigued by the pastor's method of creating a children's sermon. Each week he asks a child to take home the Sermon-in-a-Box shoebox and put something inside. The following week the pastor opens the box and builds his children's talk around whatever is inside. This particular Sunday, a couple of toothpicks reminded him of the story of David and Goliath. My friends told me he's made children's sermons out of everything from fresh fruit to teddy bears.

I marveled at what seemed to be a unique gift for finding God in the mundane and everyday. But then I began to think perhaps the gift is not in finding God in everything so much as in *looking* for Him. Anyone can find God's awesome power in the Grand Canyon, but do I even think to look for it in the lovely roses that bloom every spring outside my front door?

Or in the moment when I'm thinking of a friend with whom I've been out of touch who suddenly calls to say she was thinking of me too?

Once I began looking for God in all things, especially the tiny moments, I discovered He is everywhere in my life—in the reliable instincts of the little cactus wren who's carefully building a nest inside the tall saguaro in my front yard; in the emotional power of a sculpted angel at a nearby retreat center, such stunning beauty magically brought forth from a hunk of rock that I must stop to admire it; in the friend who offers just the right words of encouragement on a tough day. These small discoveries of God's constant presence bring great comfort. Now I try to see God every day in some small thing, and as always, He does not disappoint me.

—Gina Bridgeman

*E*VERY YEAR, AS CHRIST'S BIRTHDAY APPROACHES, there is always a magical moment when something touches our hearts with the assurance that Christmas is really coming at last. One such moment is when the great Christmas tree is lighted in Rockefeller Plaza on Fifth Avenue, jeweled with lights, flanked by towering angels made of golden wire. We love to join the hurrying throngs that always slow down to stare at the tree and the angels—especially the angels—with admiration and a touch of awe.

Why are angels so fascinating to us earthbound mortals? In this Advent season they seem to spring up everywhere: on Christmas cards and gift wrappings; in countless store windows and Nativity scenes; sometimes blowing their herald-trumpets, sometimes just sailing along "with peaceful wings unfurled."

But these are just representations, whereas the angels that appeared when Christ was born were real. They appeared to the shepherds, but they made other appearances, too, both before and after that joyous night. So as Advent comes again this year, let's turn back to the tremendous events chronicled by St. Luke and St. Matthew, and see if we can find new meaning in the various appearances of these celestial beings. Two thousand years ago they spoke clearly and directly to human beings like ourselves. Perhaps if we transport ourselves backward through time, and listen carefully and reverently, the angels also may have something to say to us this Christmas.

—Ruth Stafford Peale and Norman Vincent Peale

CHAPTER 2

Gestures
of
Comfort

❧

He maketh me to lie down in green pastures:

He leadeth me beside the still waters.

—Psalm 23:2

*M*Y HUSBAND BROUGHT HIM HOME one day in a cardboard box: a baby beagle with wistful brown eyes and Dumbo ears. I lifted him out and held him against my shoulder. From that moment the two of us became special friends.

We often sat on the grass beside the rose vine in the backyard, Murph napping while I read. Once he gnawed a rose and pricked his nose on a thorn. He looked at me so bewildered.

The children fixed a basket so Murph could ride along when I picked them up from school. But he never stayed in it. He always put his paws up to the window, wagging his tail at the scenery. But one day Murph lay in his basket and didn't get up. By evening he was very sick.

The next morning I carried him to the vet. "Better leave him with me," the vet said. Murph looked at me the way he did that day he was pricked by the thorn. The next day he died.

After the vet called, I walked outside to the rose vine, looking, I suppose, for some bit of comfort. But all the roses were dead. I could not find a single one that wasn't brown and wilted. It left me utterly sad, and when I shuffled back inside, I could hardly see through my tears.

It was noon when I heard a sound at my door. When I answered it, I saw there on the steps, a jar of fresh red roses. Beautiful *living* roses. As I gazed at them, an inexplicable comfort began to pour through me . . . a vivid sense of life's beauty and joy. I looked along the street, mystified.

Later that day my friend Betty called. "I was in the garden, praying," she told me, "when God seemed to insist that I bring you some roses."

As I hung up I was sure. No matter what thorny places we walk, God never leaves us in our pain. He sends His comfort one way or another.

—Sue Monk Kidd

WHAT A WEEK IT HAD BEEN! A huge mistake in my checkbook had caused some checks to bounce, and my paycheck was delayed. Someone smashed in the rear window of the car I'd owned for all of three weeks. Then my boss notified me that I was being laid off for six months. To say that I was depressed was an understatement!

I turned to my best friend Melodie for consolation. She seemed to be coping so well with a painful divorce and the daily stress of working full-time and raising two young boys. After listening to my litany of sorrows, she said, "You know, Tammy, when I'm about to lose it, I just go outside and look at the trees."

Trees? I looked at her as if she were nuts. But later I tried Melodie's method. And you know what? The trees did nothing for me. *But the sky was magnificent!* Huge clouds swirled amidst a multihued sunset. I found myself swept away by its beauty, and inside I began to reflect the peace I had just seen. The Creator was near and His affirming Presence just outside my door.

Are you in need of His calming Presence right now? Why not step outside and look around you? Try to find the greenest green, or the tiniest tiny, or the shiniest shiny. You may find yourself, and your life, looking up.

—Tammy Rider

*I*LEANED AGAINST THE TELEPHONE BOOTH as the tears began to fall and my body was wracked with sobs. I had just learned that I'd lost my dear friend and colleague, Glenn Kittler. Glenn had suffered with a lingering illness that required hospitalization. Then came a fatal heart attack. That Saturday afternoon, while I waited at a Westchester railroad station for a train to take me back to Manhattan, I had called the hospital to inquire about Glenn's condition. That's when I received the sad news.

The train arrived. In a daze I boarded it. As we hurtled along, bound for Grand Central Station, I stared out the window at the sparkling Hudson River. I felt so alone. I wanted desperately to talk to someone who had known Glenn, someone who could comfort me. But this was a sunny spring weekend. Many people were out of town. I didn't expect to see any of Glenn's friends until Monday morning.

Thirty-nine hours, I thought. *Thirty-nine long hours. Oh, dear God, how will I endure them?*

Finally, the train neared Grand Central, so I rose and headed toward the exit doors. As I did, I looked up and gasped. For there, coming toward me from the other end of the car was a colleague who was also a good friend of Glenn!

"Bill!" I practically shouted his name. As we talked, I learned that Bill hadn't heard about Glenn's death. And he "just happened" to be on my train.

"What a coincidence!" I said.

"Maybe not." Bill smiled as he led me to a nearby coffee shop. Together we quietly talked and prayed, remembered and grieved and found comfort in His name.

—Eleanor Sass

WHEN THE FOURTH-GRADE RELIGION CLASS at St. Matthew's Church learned that food was being wasted at Milwaukee's sports arena, they went into action. Seems that a health regulation required that all food cooked or warmed (sausages, hot dogs, pizza), or food from packages that had been opened (deli sandwiches, buns, salads, pretzels), had to be thrown out at the end of the night. So the fourth-graders wrote letters asking if the leftover food could be given to the four shelters for the homeless located within blocks of the arena.

In less than two weeks, a response came from a lawyer saying that arrangements had been worked out with the health department, so that the unused food could be given to people at the shelters after each sporting event.

What happens to the leftover food at the restaurants, sports arenas, movie houses and concession stands in your town? Could you be the one to find out and perhaps start the wheels in motion for getting that food to the hungry? Today, why not call your favorite restaurant and ask what is done with their leftover food each night. Could you be the one to pick it up and deliver it to a shelter for the homeless one night a week? Could you find half a dozen friends to help you?

—Patricia Lorenz

WHENEVER I GET DISCOURAGED about human nature, I get out my file of newspaper clippings about ordinary people who've shown compassion for others. It heals my heart. For example, in a January 1971 story, I read about eleven-year-old Dean Herron, who took his entire savings of seventy-five dollars to a sheriff's auction, hoping to buy back his three runaway ponies. Dean had bought the ponies with money earned from scrubbing floors, and they were his special friends until a snowmobile broke the fence and they got out. Deputies spent six hours retrieving the ponies. The animals had already cost the county four hundred dollars when a public auction was ordered. "Do I hear a bid of thirty dollars?" asked the judge, pointing to the first pony. The boy stepped forward and gasped, "Thirty dollars! That's too much. You should start at twenty-five."

"Are you bidding?" asked the judge.

"They're *my ponies!*" the boy cried.

A conference was held between the judge and the animal-shelter direc-tor and bidding was reopened on all three ponies "as a package." A friend of the family entered the boy's bid of seventy-five dollars. Young Herron looked anxiously around at the others who had come to bid, but not another voice was heard. "Mr. Herron," the judge said to the boy with the tears in his eyes, "you've just bought yourself some ponies!"

Maybe you'd like to start a file of "compassion stories," too. It will keep the cynic out of you!

—Marilyn Morgan Helleberg

M Y NINE-YEAR-OLD DAUGHTER KAREN woke up one Saturday night with great pain in her right foot. The next morning we took her to the doctor for X rays. After seeing two more doctors, it was determined that Karen might have cancer.

After six weeks of tests, my wife Roe and I were sitting in a waiting room while a surgeon in a New York City hospital performed a bone biopsy on Karen. The doctor said he could determine if Karen had a tumor and if the tumor was cancer.

That was the longest two-hour wait Roe and I have endured in our married years together. We didn't tell Karen of the potential threat. All she knew was that we were trying to find out what was wrong with her foot.

Karen was allowed to bring her stuffed toy dog with her into the operating room. After the surgery, the doctor came to us with the good news that Karen did not have a tumor and she would be fine—a stress fracture they discovered would eventually heal itself. Roe and I stepped into the recovery room to find Karen still asleep. Sitting at her side was her stuffed dog wearing a green surgical mask and cap.

Perhaps the doctors will never know what that small act of kindness and humor meant to me and to my family. The playfully dressed dog told us others were watching over our daughter and caring for her, too, and it comforted our spirits.

—Christopher de Vinck

*I*N EARLY JUNE, the little town of Cave Springs, Georgia, welcomes visitors to its annual arts festival. Between a cave where pure water gushes and a free-flowing river where trout hide from barefoot fishermen, a host of artisans set up their tents in the public park.

Wandering through the festival's art display, I stopped before a painting of an old raw-board farmhouse. The house's sagging front porch was heaped with presents: bicycles, a scooter, several boxes of groceries. In the midst of it all, a small boy with a red cowboy hat perched on his head was dancing.

As I puzzled over the painting, the artist approached me. "My daddy had left us some months before," he explained softly. "Mamma didn't think we'd have a Christmas. But I was a little fellow, and I couldn't help praying and believing. When I peeped out the window on Christmas morning, there were all those presents. We never knew who left them, but the feeling of dancing across the porch in that new red hat has stayed with me. Sooner or later, I just had to paint it."

The impact of that painting just won't let me go: Someone out there performed an anonymous act of kindness on a long ago night, a good deed that lives on and reaches out from an artist's canvas.

For those of us who haven't yet accepted Jesus' invitation to give in secret without fanfare or thanks, this illustration of selfless giving poses an interesting question: Might some barren porch or hopeful heart be waiting for my touch? Has God stretched an empty canvas somewhere near, where I can quietly, anonymously, paint His love?

—Pam Kidd

*L*AST THURSDAY OUR FRIEND RUXANDRA, or "Ruxy" as she is fondly called, brought her forty-nine-year-old husband Donald home from the hospital to die. Donald had fought cancer valiantly for more than a year; now he knew his departure from this world would be a matter of a few days or weeks.

This Monday I found myself constantly thinking of them. I yearned to help, but I didn't want to intrude on their last days together. Although I had talked and worked with Ruxy at church, I hardly knew Donald. I had spoken with him only a few times. Besides, what could I possibly do?

Then I remembered something I'd once heard: "When the only thing you can do is pray, then that's the most important thing to do—and it will make a difference!"

So I began praying for my friends and found myself asking God to send

His angels to help them. I pictured invisible heavenly beings whispering comfort to them, easing Donald's pain and strengthening Ruxy to care for him.

On Wednesday my nurse friend Barb said that Ruxy had called her with several questions. "I've got tomorrow off," said Barb, "so I'm going to visit them." *Ah,* I thought, *one of God's angels!*

That evening our friend Mary phoned and said that she had called Ruxy. "She's been getting very little sleep, so I'm going over there now to take the night shift."

"Oh, Mary," I said, "you're another angel God is sending them!"

"Oh, no," she protested, "you know I am no angel. But please pray for us—that I'll be able to care for him alone and Ruxy will be able to sleep."

"I will," I promised, grateful for a way to help.

That night as I prayed, I pictured Mary ministering to Donald and Ruxy sleeping peacefully, watched over by God's angels.

—Mary Brown

ARLY ON A SATURDAY MORNING, my husband and I woke up in a lovely, old-fashioned bed-and-breakfast room. We were due at a prayer breakfast in what seemed a very short time. I took the plunge, jumped out of bed and ran over to the window. There was snow—lots of it—and our car, parked beneath the window, looked like an igloo. "Edward, get up," I urged. "We don't even have a scraper."

We began to get ready in disgruntled haste, not at all the right frame of mind for gathering to pray. And I was responsible for the opening words.

Suddenly, I heard an odd rhythmic noise, like a distant lawn mower. Hairbrush in hand, I walked over to the window. There below me was the hooded figure of a fellow guest whose acquaintance we had made only briefly the night before. As quietly as he could, he was cleaning the snow off our car windows. He had already finished his own car parked next to ours.

I drew a deep breath as I let the curtain fall into place. Someone, almost a stranger, without fuss was smoothing our path that early morning. Scraper in hand, he was loving his neighbor in practical fashion. Clearly he planned to drive off unseen. I had no difficulty with that day's opening prayer, entitled, as it happened, "For Others."

—Brigitte Weeks

*A*BOUT TWENTY YEARS AGO I began corresponding with a woman I'll call Ryan. We didn't actually meet until about five years ago, when she moved to the Atlanta area. We met for lunch and occasionally dropped each other notes. After a while she mentioned almost casually in a letter that for some time she'd been sleeping in her car.

Her needs were overwhelming. My initial reaction was to put some distance between us, but I tried to do the best I could for her. I made countless calls, trying to find her a place to live and help of some kind. I continued to write to her, enclosing what assistance I could. It's very difficult to share the little happenings of everyday life with someone who's living out of a car.

Ryan always answered my letters in her beautiful handwriting, insisting that God was meeting her needs. When her children were small, her minister-husband had left them. Later, a horrific storm had taken away her house and belongings. But she insisted that God was still with her and took care of her. "I'm sleeping in the Waldorf-Astoria of parking lots! A policeman—or maybe he's an angel—watches over me." One note said, "What you sent was just what I needed today." *What about the other days?* I wondered.

My help was so insignificant and my sense of discomfort so great that I thought about not writing. Then a letter came. "I don't tell people how I live anymore," Ryan wrote. "They are too uncomfortable with my situation and turn away."

Whenever I had read the story of Jesus' Crucifixion, I had always felt anger at the disciples who ran away and hid. *I would have been there with John and the two Marys,* I had thought, *not hiding in the courtyard like Peter.* Now I knew better. I went to my typewriter and wrote, "Dear Ryan . . ."

—Marion Bond West

*W*HEN ANDREA AND I WERE FIRST MARRIED, our relationship was beautiful. We could tell each other anything, it seemed. We enjoyed being together all the time. We promised ourselves that we would always work hard to keep things that way.

But one day several years later, everything seemed about to fall apart. We could hardly talk about the changes without becoming angry and afraid. Without saying it out loud, we knew that our conscious feelings of love had definitely subsided. Since we both went to church and prayed regularly, we couldn't imagine how it had happened.

When we married, Andrea was marketing director for a large music company. She is a very competent manager, and she seemed to enjoy getting my office and vocational life organized. But as the years passed, she wanted to try her hand at her own business. As she got more and more involved in it, she had less and less time to help me. I felt like a deserted little boy inside, and I couldn't get nearly as much work done as I had before. When Andrea saw me floundering, she felt guilty.

The thing that saved us was our spiritual discipline of prayer and our commitment to share our feelings honestly with each other, even if it was scary to do so. I finally told Andrea that I was having feelings of being deserted. She expressed her fear of not being able to try her vocational wings. We discussed how we could rearrange the way we approached our two jobs and hire the help we needed to move ahead. And to our surprise, our feelings of love and caring for each other came back.

To me, this conversation was one of God's miracles. As we both listened and honestly expressed our understanding of the other's feelings, we suddenly knew that with God's help we could work out a way that we could both do the work we felt He was calling us to do.

—Keith Miller

M Y HUSBAND WAS PERFORMING in a musical at a local college, and I decided to attend. "You can read while you wait," he said. "The doors will open in about twenty minutes."

Finding a comfortable spot, I propped my purse by my feet and took out a paperback. My reading was interrupted by the two girls sitting next to me.

"Oh, he's just so totally real. Like, really, he's like too much, you know? It's like, like, awesome."

Her friend responded, "Yes, really cool. I know what you mean. Like, how wild. Like, too much. You know, like, I mean really. It's like, really way out."

Is this the way college students converse with each other? I wondered. *They need a course in communication.* I promised myself never to use the word *like* again.

At last the doors opened, and I went inside to claim my seat. After settling in and making myself comfortable, I reached for my purse. With a sinking feeling, I realized it wasn't there. I got up and ran out to the lobby. No purse. It was gone! Without much hope, I went to ask at the reception desk, though I thought my purse must be halfway across campus by now.

"Did anyone turn in a purse?" I asked.

"Yes," the young man replied. "The two girls sitting next to you found it after you left." He handed it to me.

"The girls?" I queried. "The ones sitting next to me?"

Those lovely girls. Those, like, totally awesome girls.

—Susan Schefflein

*A*N ELDERLY LADY IN OUR TOWN passed on a pile of old songbooks to me and I spent some happy hours going through them. I felt a responsive chord tug at the sight of the song "Transformed" by Mrs. F. G. Burroughs, which had consoled me when I was a young boy:

> *Dear Lord, take up the tangled strands,*
> *where we have wrought in vain.*
> *That by the skill of Thy dear hands,*
> *some beauty may remain.*

I don't have the slightest idea what my problems were at twelve, but I do remember poor health making my life a bundle of tangled strands early on. In college I got all fired up to serve in Tibet, but a missionary board physician turned me down as too weak—three times. I looked closer to home for a mission and happily found it. And later, in the mid-1970s, I was called on a three-month mission to Vietnam to serve Christian lay pastors just before the fall of Saigon. God had untangled my tangled strands and allowed me to serve Him in what capacity He thought best.

Today, in my retirement years, I still run into tangled strands—decreasing mobility, waning energy. But I hold them up to the Lord in prayer, and trust Him to show me the beauty of each day. There are books that feed my understanding; nature walks with their seasonal lessons about life; grandchildren who need encouragement; young seminary students who seek my advice. There are quiet moments to be still, and deep, late-evening talks with my wife. And always there is the joy of each waking moment in communion with my Lord.

—Lee Webber

NOT LONG AGO a friend told me about a teacher who made a remarkable impression on him. One afternoon he was walking down the school hallway when one of his classmates dropped a jar of ink. Dark blue puddles oozed across a wooden floor that had just been carefully sanded and refinished.

The boy froze. His teacher had warned him to leave the ink at his desk. He lowered his head and prepared for the harsh words he was sure would follow. The teacher, whose face had registered shock when she looked at the floor, looked in sympathy at the boy, whose face had gone pale.

"Why, doesn't that look like a butterfly!" she exclaimed. "Too bad we can't leave it there. Why don't you go find some towels and I'll help you clean it up."

My friend says he remembers that incident every time something goes wrong. I think I will, too. It helps me realize that mistakes are best erased . . . with love.

—Terry Helwig

I STOOD WATCHING in a marine tourist shop. For a small sum of money, customers could select an oyster, have it opened and keep the pearl inside. One child's eyes widened when the attendant laid a cream-colored pearl, about the size of a kernel of corn, into her palm. I marveled at the oyster's ability to produce a pearl from an irritating grain of sand by covering it with layers of nacre, also called mother-of-pearl.

I remember one morning, some years ago, when my husband Jim and I discovered that someone had tried to break into our brand-new home. The shiny dead-bolt lock had held, though it was bent, and part of the door had splintered. Even though the damage was minor, we were distressed at the senseless invasion.

The locksmith shook his head when I told him what happened. After an hour's work, he proudly showed me the new lock. And, with even more pride, he told me he wasn't going to charge me. Then the carpenter came and he, too, said there would be no charge. "You've just moved into the area," he explained. "And I'd like to show you some hospitality." After those two men left, I felt truly blessed.

Upon reflection I think I have much to learn from the oyster. Sometimes, life's little irritations are actually opportunities . . . for making pearls.

—Terry Helwig

WHEN I WAS VERY YOUNG, I was enchanted by angels: Michael with his great wings and flaming sword . . . pastel-winged Gabriel standing in the presence of the Lord . . . my guardian angel . . . heavenly hosts. Everywhere I went I listened expectantly, and sometimes I even heard the rustle of wings.

Then I grew up. I forgot all about angels—until one day recently. I was expecting a beloved friend to visit. My yard was not fit to receive anyone. Somehow, in the press of other work, I hadn't noticed that the hedge had become a forest, the weeds were in full bloom, the lawn was a full-fledged meadow. Ruefully I sighed, "Well, I can cook, Lord, but I'll have to leave the gardening to you."

That afternoon a courteous youth and his father appeared at my door. They were looking for a yard to "do." And they "did" mine—to perfection.

I took their phone number and later called it, hoping to thank them. There was no answer.

"Well," I surprised myself by thinking, "maybe angels don't answer phones!" And I never saw nor heard from the pair again.

Now I try to be more expectant, watching for the "angels" who pass through my daily life. And I'm content to accept them as such—without wings, without questions, but with a heart full of thanksgiving.

—Elaine St. Johns

ONE OF OUR 4-H CLUB SERVICE PROJECTS was cleaning Colusa Cemetery. Each May, kids and parents with rakes, hoes and mowers would spend a hard, hot afternoon getting the little country cemetery spruced up for Memorial Day. My children usually complained about the waste of time. Secretly, I felt the same way. No one had been buried there for twenty years; most families now had plots in Copeland, Kansas. Besides, Colusa was practically hidden by cornfields. No one ever saw it.

Then I received a letter requesting a strange favor. "My grandfather, George Wolfe, is in poor health," the writer explained. "Years ago his parents were traveling through Kansas when their baby girl was born and died. Grandfather thinks his sister was buried at Copeland sometime between 1906 and 1910. Her name was Dora or Doris. Could you check?"

"I'll try," I wrote back. But when I looked at the Copeland Cemetery roll book, my heart sank. Copeland hadn't opened until 1921. That meant the child was in one of the dozens of township and family cemeteries in the area. Ivanhoe, Lockport and, of course, Colusa had been kept up, but little remained of many others. But I'd promised to look, so a week later I took my camera and started the search. To my amazement, I located the tiny granite headstone right away—in the northeast corner of Colusa Cemetery. The inscription was worn but legible:

DORIS—Infant daughter
of
W.M. & Leota Wolfe

Thanks to the work of generations of 4-H'ers, the weeds had been pulled from around the headstone and the grass neatly mowed. I sent Mr. Wolfe a picture of the grave he's never seen. His letter of thanks changed my attitude about cemetery cleanup and Memorial Day. Someone remembers, and Someone sees.

—Penney Schwab

*A*s Parkinson's disease continued to devastate my husband Bob, we realized we would need an electric hospital bed at home for him. They're far from cheap, and with other medical expenses taking a big chunk of our income, purchasing one seemed impossible.

"We can't give up," our daughter Emily said during a winter visit. "Let's all pray for a way to be opened for him to have one."

No change in our circumstances occurred until a day in April. A fellow employee in the insurance company where Emily works, called her into her office. "This is Mrs. Walton," she told Emily. "I think you two have something in common. You need an electric hospital bed, and she has one she wants to get rid of."

"How much are you asking for it?" Emily asked.

"I don't want to sell it," Mrs. Walton answered. "I want to give it to someone who can use it. It was my husband's, and since his death, I've been looking for someone to give it to."

Emily recognized the bed as a gift from God. That's what she called it when she phoned to tell us about it. And when a truck from Emily's office brought it to our house, I knew it was, too.

—Drue Duke

O
N MONDAY, I HAD A BIOPSY as an outpatient at Good Samaritan
Hospital here in Kearney, Nebraska. I prayed that Jesus would watch
over me and I was quite calm about it all, until I got into the pre-op room
and several nurses started working on me, placing an IV in my arm, monitor tabs on my chest and a hypo in my hip.

As I felt my heart beginning to race, a quiet, dark-haired woman with
soft brown eyes took hold of my hand. "My name is Julie," she said, "and
I'll be with you throughout your surgery and until you're ready to go
home." Then Julie very carefully explained to me exactly what to expect
when I was wheeled into the operating room, what would happen there,
that I'd have an oxygen mask on when I woke up, and that she'd take it off
as soon as I was able to tell her where I was and the day of the week.

My hand was in Julie's as I went under the anesthetic and also when I was coming out of it. I can't tell you what a comfort that was! And thanks be to God, the biopsy showed no evidence of cancer.

Jesus promised that He would be with me throughout this life, and I know He was there that day. When I'm frightened or insecure about anything, I can always turn within to hear that gentle voice saying, "My name is Jesus, and I'm with you in this all the way."

—Marilyn Morgan Helleberg

*I*T HAD BEEN ONE OF THOSE DAYS! With so much to do before houseguests arrived, I got out of bed in the morning, running. Now it was
the middle of the hot summer afternoon, and I was sweeping the sidewalk
and mentally enumerating the remaining chores to be done before dark.
From his sandbox next door, my two-year-old neighbor Tyler came
running.

After his usual, "Whatcha doing?" he said, "Let's swing in your swing."

"I'm too busy today," I told him.

Disappointment spread over his face. I glanced toward the swing hanging in the breezeway and saw it move gently in the light breeze. It *did* look
inviting.

"All right," I told him. "Just for a few minutes."

He raced up the front steps and waited for me to lift him into the swing beside me. He didn't talk, just snuggled against me as my toe made the swing glide to and fro. A butterfly fluttered past my face. Two bees hummed among the flowers and a slight breeze stroked my tired body. Tension and anxiety began to slip away. Soon I was humming softly. I became aware of the fragrance of the flowers, the brilliance of the day, the wonder of the small boy beside me, all creations of a loving God. . . .

On those days when you become entangled in a maze of activities and overwhelmed by all that you are called upon to do, go and find a quiet spot where you can get away for a while. Relax, think about Him and let His unending strength and peace refresh you.

—Drue Duke

M Y FRIEND ANNE went to hear Edith Schaeffer, the Christian writer and lecturer. The speaker was swamped by people having her autograph their books. Everyone had brought their lunch, and Anne sat down to eat hers. All she had brought was a large, red apple. As she looked over at the author busily signing books, she felt a sudden impulse to give the apple to Edith. Feeling a bit self-conscious, she got up and laid the apple on the table. Then she hurried away without speaking.

"Come back, please come back," Edith called out loudly.

Even more embarrassed, Anne went back. Edith said, "Last night in my hotel room I so longed for a red, juicy apple that today my Father has given it to me through you. Thank you."

As Anne told me this story, tears splashed down her face. "You won't believe what happened next," she continued. "When I went back to join my friends one of them said, 'Anne, where have you been? I brought you something.' Then she handed me this tremendous red, shiny apple!

"But that's not all. The next day someone sent us a huge basket of the choicest apples grown anywhere. Isn't it amazing how even the tiniest kindness can come back—multiplied!"

—Marion Bond West

The Power

of

Love

∿

He restoreth my soul....

—Psalm 23:3

WHEN DAD WAS GETTING MOM settled back home after her stroke, I was unsure of how best to assist them. I went nervously to work, clearing the living room of excess furniture to accommodate Mom's wheel-chair. I was quite alarmed when Dad said, "We're picking up a new puppy on Monday."

The last thing he needs is a new puppy, I thought, *chewing up every bag in the garage and getting underfoot when Dad is backing the wheelchair through the front door.*

Dad read the look on my face and said meekly, "I've already promised the owner I'd take her."

I immediately added a new task to my list: Go to the junk store and buy a playpen to corral a four-footed, yelping cyclone. I didn't find a playpen, and I was upset that I hadn't been able to save Dad from the nuisance of a new, untrained puppy.

The next week when I telephoned Mom, she told me that they'd named the puppy Princess. It had been terribly frustrating trying to communicate with Mom over the phone, but suddenly there was one subject on which Mom could always manage to make sense: Princess and her antics. And the next time I drove up to visit, Mom was sitting in the yard with Princess on her lap. We sat and watched as Princess bounded over the blooming purple thrift and caught a butterfly. I was astounded when Mom laughed out loud, something she hadn't done in years.

I leaned over and gave Princess a pat on her sandy, curly head, thinking I'd learned my first lesson in parenting my parents: I'm sometimes wrong about what's good for them. Just as I do with my own children, I need to trust them—and trust God that they can make good decisions without my dictating what I think is best.

—Karen Barber

WHEN I WAS FOUR, my Southern family of grandmother, aunts, uncles, cousins, along with my immediate family, gathered for a reunion in a large beach house on St. Simons Island off the coast of Georgia. When it came time to leave, no one seemed to realize my misery at not being able to stay at the ocean. I felt so happy there.

But, I discovered, someone did realize. As Mother, Dad, John and I headed for our car to drive the two hundred miles inland to Macon, Rosa took me aside. Rosa, the large, quiet, smiling cook, handed me a bag, saying, "Here, missy, this is for you."

The little brown bag was full of beautiful shells—memories to take home with me. She'd awakened early to gather them before making breakfast. Somehow in my childish mind I knew her act of kindness to be much more important than anything I'd yet received.

Rosa wasn't wealthy, but she was perceptive and willing to go out of her way to make someone else happy—and those, I realized as I gazed at the shells from throughout my childhood, were the essentials for gift giving.

—Samantha McGarrity

*M*USKETS FIRED ON BOTH SIDES. Kirkland's commanding officer granted his request. But, regretfully, he would not be allowed to wave a white flag. If Kirkland climbed over the wall, he would have to take his chances. But he had to go, he could no longer endure the cries of "water" coming from the wounded on the battlefield. He lowered his weapon, hoisted several canteens over the shoulder of his Confederate uniform and scurried from behind the protective wall.

The muskets fell silent as Kirkland knelt beside a wounded soldier—an enemy soldier. He lifted the soldier's head and tilted the canteen toward his lips. Kirkland then removed his own coat and laid it across the soldier's body.

Cheers rang out from the Northern side. The South joined in. For an hour and a half, Kirkland carried water to the dying and wounded. Every time he disappeared behind the wall to refill his canteens, the musket-fire resumed on both sides. But every time he reappeared, the firing ceased and the cheering began again.

The story of Sergeant Kirkland, who later became known as "The Angel of Marye's Heights," moves me. For it boldly embodies Christ's compassionate spirit. Kirkland's compassion ran deeper than patriotic loyalty or the fear of losing his life. Perhaps the hearts of the truly compassionate recognize that the cry of the enemy and the cry of a brother sound very much the same.

—Terry Helwig

*M*Y WIFE SHARON AND I had a shouting match, and she fled the room in tears, while I went grimly back to my wallpapering.

All at once my foot caught the rim of the sponge bucket, and water spilled onto the hardwood floor. I seized a large rag to halt the growing pond, then stopped and stared. The rag was one of Sharon's old dresses, one of my favorites. She always was so beautiful, like an Irish queen, in that burgundy plaid with the snow-white collar and cuffs.

Slowly the old fabric sopped up the pasty water and turned to a dark, ugly shadow on the floor. As I gazed at the soggy garment, my eyes filled with tears. God was using this object to show me how I was using my own precious wife to "sop up my frustrations."

There's an old saying: "You always hurt the one you love." I know. I'm guilty occasionally of forgetting kindnesses and courtesies, because I'm short-tempered or frustrated and my partner is the nearest target. But I'm learning. . . .

When Sharon awoke from her nap, I peeked into the bedroom. "I'm sorry," I whispered. "I didn't mean to yell. I'm just very tired. I love you."

She smiled, and I was forgiven.

—Daniel Schantz

*M*Y GRANDFATHER WAS NOT A DEMONSTRATIVE MAN, and I don't recall ever climbing into his lap or hugging him. Even at a young age I knew that would be inappropriate. But one day he took me into his vegetable garden.

That side-yard garden couldn't have been very big, but to me it was a miracle. Corn towered over my head; pea pods dangled at eye-level; I had to take giant steps over the lettuce. We walked in silence, as always, except for his recitation of "corn . . . peas . . . lettuce" as he pointed to each vegetable. There was never idle chatter with him. Suddenly he hunkered down, pulled a tiny carrot up by its top, dusted it off and held it out to me. "Your mother'd like that washed, but it's better with a little dirt." He motioned impatiently. "Eat it!"

I had never tasted anything so sweet in my life! We ate our way through raw carrots, peas, lettuce and other vegetables, all in silence. Then it was over.

That brusque, cool man changed my life that summer day. With no fuss or bother, he'd shown me that he did indeed love me, pest that I was. He taught me that love can be shown in ways other than words or hugs. He taught me to see far more than the joys of a garden.

He's long gone now, but I still plant carrots for him each spring.

—Toni Sortor

*B*EING A WIDOW WITH TEENAGED BOYS was harder than I'd expected. My sons resented the fact that I was in charge. Sometimes I did, too.

Late one afternoon, one of my sons announced that he was going to a party he knew I'd disapprove of. I told him that he couldn't go. "I'm going anyway," Jon said defiantly. I was so tired of arguing—and then I remembered God's promise to be a husband to widows. I silently asked Him for help and thought I understood the instructions that crept into my heart. I rushed to the front porch, waved happily at my son and called out, "I'm putting some angels in the back of your truck, Jon!"

He leaned out the window. "Can you do that?" he asked with sarcasm, but I walked back to the kitchen and enjoyed the delicious flavor of *not* being in charge. God was up to something! Jon returned home shortly and stood in the kitchen watching me cook. Finally, he said, "I decided not to go to the party. What's for supper?"

I refrained from doing cartwheels across the kitchen. After a pleasant supper, Jon said, half serious, half smiling, "Mother, I'm probably the only boy in Georgia with angels in the back of his truck. Would you . . . could you arrange for them to leave now?" His eye contact was good, his voice gentle.

"Certainly," I replied, smiling. I took off my apron and walked out to the porch, as though I dispatched angels on a daily routine. Jon followed. I waved toward the truck. "Thank you all very much. That's all for now. Bye."

—Marion Bond West

*M*R. WITCHEL WAS EIGHTY and, because of his experience, charged a high fee to tune our piano. My husband and I would have paid it gladly, but the upper octaves of our piano still sounded like sour lemons.

We complained and Mr. Witchel reworked it. It wasn't any better. In fact, he denied that anything was wrong. But to placate us, he agreed to bring another tuner for a second opinion.

The second tuner, a man of fifty, agreed with Mr. Witchel that the piano was perfect. Suspecting collaboration, we angrily ordered them out of the house.

Half an hour later, the second tuner returned, bag in hand.

"You're right about those high notes," he admitted. "But you see, Elmer's hearing is going." He shook his head sadly. "He taught me how to tune pianos and for sixty years he has lived for tuning. I just can't tell this man, my friend, that his life is over."

He corrected the tuning free, asking us to keep it a secret.

Elmer Witchel is gone now, so he can't be hurt if I share this simple story. I think of him often, and of his friend, too, knowing that this is the kind of love Jesus wants me to show—a love that preserves the dignity of a friend.

—Dee Ann Palmer

*I*N MY EARLY TWENTIES I wrote a Christmas play that was published in a magazine. Shortly thereafter, I received a phone call from a Sunday-school superintendent. "We would like our junior high group to put on your play, and we're wondering if you'd direct it for us."

I'd never directed anything in my life, and Christmas was only six weeks away. But the superintendent said that they would get the costumes and assign the parts. All I had to do was show up.

I did. And what I found terrified me: fifteen seventh- and eighth-graders jumping over benches, throwing paper airplanes, shouting, laughing. The rehearsal was abysmal. The kids wouldn't settle down. Joseph, a big guy with flaming red hair, was the ringleader. Clowning, making faces, he egged the others on. The only one who was serious about her part was Mary, a sweet, brown-eyed girl with long hair.

"If these kids don't settle down, we're not going to be able to do the play," I said to the other teachers at the end of the evening.

"Let's pray," the superintendent said. So, forming a circle and holding hands, she led us in a prayer for a miracle.

Two more awful rehearsals passed. The teachers and I reasoned, threatened, pleaded. We now had only three weeks until the play, and I was ready to quit. But each time the superintendent said, "Let's pray. God can work a miracle."

And so He did. At the fourth rehearsal, Joseph was transformed. He'd fallen in love with Mary. Shuffling and awkward, he gazed adoringly at her and she at him. Paper airplanes ceased to fly. Everyone, from shepherds to angels to wise men, followed Joseph's lead and pulled their acts together.

We'd asked for a miracle; we got one. But, as so often happens, God made it out of what was already there: a boy, a girl and adolescent hormones.

—Shari Smyth

*I*T WAS AN INVITATION to fault-finding: a mother-in-law with an advanced degree in child-development and years at a children's clinic; a daughter-in-law who'd never so much as seen a jar of baby food. I was almost unbelievably innocent of household skills, let alone the care of a baby.

Before the birth of our first child, I enrolled in a course for new mothers, but even among fellow beginners I was sadly ignorant. The other women had questions about diaper pails and diaper services, while I wished the instructor would simply hold up a diaper so I could see what one looked like.

And it was to this woefully unprepared young woman that Mother Sherrill's first grandchild was born. She would look down at little John Scott in his bassinet ("What's a bassinet?" I'd asked in class), noting, I was sure, half a dozen things amiss. Too many blankets? Gown on backward? Underpad bunched up? And Mother Sherill would say, "How comfortable he looks!"

Bathing, diet, feeding schedule, in every aspect of my mothering she found something to like, something to praise. Each time she left our little apartment I'd feel sure her tongue must hurt from biting it. Certainly, I wasn't doing things as she would have done.

But each time she left I'd feel, too, that I was a bit more skilled, a bit more competent than I'd imagined. Not corrected by her expertise, however excellent, but growing into motherhood in the kindly sunshine of her approval.

—Elizabeth Sherrill

"OH, YOU'RE SUCH A SAINT!" How my mother dreaded hearing those words. Yet hear them she did as soon as anyone found out that she was a foster parent who cared for over forty children, many of them handicapped. "I'm no saint," she'd protest to me in private. I'd nod in agreement; she was a normal mother to me, occasionally losing her patience, often a caring and supportive friend.

One day someone told me the story of a little boy who was asked in Sunday school to define a saint. The little boy thought hard, then remembered the stained glass windows in the sanctuary, the ones depicting various saints. "A saint," he answered, "is a person the light shines through!"

That definition was true of my mother, and it can be true for each one of us. We can let God's light shine through us. Today, perhaps you can take the time to talk with the stranger in the checkout line, the one who reveals that she and her husband have just moved to town. Or perhaps you'll find a way to be patient when a child asks "Why?" for the umpteenth time. I'm going to find a way to let my faith shine, and I know you will, too.

—Tammy Rider

FOR ALMOST A YEAR my eleven-year-old son Jeremy had begged to have a hamster. I'd said no because we already had so many pets at home. A few weeks after Christmas I was surprised to find that Jeremy was reading from his Bible every day. When I asked him about it, he told me that he managed to read four chapters at a time. I was amazed. He'd never done that before. "And I pray, too," he said. "One of my prayers is that you'll let me have a hamster."

I was so touched I said, "Well, maybe I'll have to reconsider."

"Really, Mama? Really?" he said.

I nodded, but almost immediately regretted having made such a statement. Hamsters always seemed too much like rats. I couldn't stand them. Then at a luncheon one day, mothers were talking about children and pets. I said resignedly, "I may let my son have a hamster." Across the table a mother's face lit up. "Oh, please let him have Missy's. She loves him but has grown tired of caring for him. She's praying for a good home for Sam, where someone will love him."

A few days later I took Jeremy over to meet Sam. Sam made some noises that almost sounded like he was speaking. Jeremy held him close, asking Missy's mother questions like, "How old is he?" "Is he healthy?" "Are you sure you want to give him away?" "Do you think he likes me?"

When we drove home with Sam, Jeremy said, "My heart is about to beat out. I already love him, but I'm gonna rename him Cooper, like the dog in that book I read. Do you think that's okay?"

I assured him that I liked the name Cooper. Funny thing, I was even beginning to like the little hamster.

What a God, I later marvelled. He heard a little girl praying for a home for her pet, and He heard a little boy praying for his mama to let him have a hamster. And He worked out all the details.

—Marion Bond West

WHERE TIGER CAME FROM we'll never know, nor where he goes when we're away. He simply sprang from the hedges one night when we drove in from our weekend at the lake; a striped gray tom, howling as if to demand, "Where have you *been?*" and entwining our legs like long-lost kin.

Because of our two dogs, we fed and bedded Tiger on the porch, thinking he'd surely be gone in a few days. But he promptly took up residence. And our instant, abiding love for him has never waned.

So it was with some regret that we left for a month's vacation that first year. Margaret, our next-door neighbor, agreed to feed him, but we doubted Tiger would be there when we returned. And sure enough it was true.

"Sorry about your cat," Margaret told us. "He hung around for a couple of days, then disappeared."

But as we stood mourning the inevitable, who should come scurrying up to purr his forgiveness and welcome but Tiger?

And thus it has been for almost four years. Mysteriously, he senses our homecoming. And no matter how long we may have stayed away, he comes rushing upon us, showing in every way he can how much he loves us, and how glad he is to have us home. And, no matter how far from the Father we stray, or how long we may be gone, He always faithfully awaits our return.

—Marjorie Holmes

*A*S THEY MADE THE FINAL TURN into the homestretch, two runners had left the others far behind. Striding side by side, it was anyone's guess which of the two hard-charging teenagers would get to the finish line first. Then the girl on the inside tripped and fell, making the other runner a certain victor.

But that's not what happened. When the sure winner saw her rival go down, she did something startling, something no one watching had ever seen before. She quit the race and ran back to help her fallen comrade, who as it turns out wasn't hurt. Meanwhile, all the other runners passed them and finished the race.

Hardly anyone noticed who won. That's because all eyes were on the two girls at the head of the stretch. Smiling and laughing, they resumed running, locked arm-in-arm. And when they finished together, tied for last, the crowd greeted them with the loudest applause of the day.

This incident happened several years ago during the Special Olympics competition, conducted for young people with learning disabilities. Wouldn't it be nice if the girl who gave up glory to help someone else could teach us all to see things as clearly.

—Fred Bauer

*G*OD GAVE ME A GIFT TODAY. It was originally a gift *from* me, a needle-point tote bag I made for my mother-in-law. Nothing remarkable, except that I had never before (or since) done anything with a needle. Knitting, embroidery, sewing of any kind in my fingers became a hopeless snarl.

But Mother Sherrill loved handmade things, so when my friend Mavis Hart found me this simple kit, I started in. It was a matter of stitching colored yarns through a plastic webbing of big, kindergarten-size mesh. I labored on it month after month, picturing Mother's surprise when her daughter-in-law presented her with this proof of domestic skills.

It took me three years to complete. And by then tragedy had come to our family. My brilliant mother-in-law, a lecturer and writer, was in an institution, diagnosed with arteriosclerosis, living in an unreachable private world, her memory gone. When her son, my husband John, would fly down to Louisville, Kentucky, to see her, she'd mistake him for the doctor. Family, friends, her long distinguished career, all forgotten.

John took the tote bag to her anyway. "Tib made this for you, Mother," he told her, using my nickname, though of course she wouldn't remember me.

Mother turned the bag over and over in her hands. "Tib made it?" she asked. "But Tib doesn't sew!"

It was a flash of real contact, a momentary connection, brought on no doubt by the shock of the totally unexpected. From that day on, nurses reported, each time a visitor came Mother would hold up the needlepoint bag. "Tib made this!"

Since Mother's death, the bag has hung on a hook in my closet, where it caught my eye this morning. Welcome surprises, it told me. God connects with us through the unexpected, too!

—Elizabeth Sherrill

127

*I*N 1970, I VOLUNTEERED AS A PLAY LADY at Boston Children's Hospital. Most often I read stories, drew cartoons or helped with crafts that could be done in bed. Sometimes I would play quiet games to calm an overly excited child who had thrown his slippers across the ward as he awaited a tonsillectomy. At other times, I would use puppets to cheer up a teary child who'd been confined to her bed for weeks or months, or just stop to admire a child's get-well cards. My repertoire varied, but I could always find something to share with the children.

One sultry summer evening, I walked into the last room on my list and found a toddler prone in his crib in the twilight. His head was wrapped in bandages, and an IV tube was dripping fluids into his leg. He didn't raise his head to look at me when I spoke to him. I sang a couple of lullabies. No response.

Oh, well, I thought, *there's not much I can do here. I may as well go home.*

I stroked the child's tiny forearm, gave his little hand a gentle squeeze good-bye—and then froze. The little guy seemed to be squeezing back.

I tried squeezing in a pattern: *squeeze, squeeze, pause.* Sure enough, he squeezed back: *squeeze, squeeze, pause.* I tried another pattern: *squeeze, pause, squeeze, pause.* Again the little boy, who couldn't even turn his head, mimicked me. We continued our game for many minutes, without words, without eye contact.

When I finally left for the night, I felt ashamed that I had nearly given up on a tiny being who had needs that could not be spoken, and grateful to God for using one so helpless to teach me a lesson in love.

—Gail Thorell Schilling

I'LL NEVER GET ANOTHER DOG," my friend Deborah said when her beloved dog died. "The loss is too painful." A lot of people feel that way when they lose a pet. Nevertheless, when you love animals, it's hard to live without them, and Deborah just wasn't smiling anymore.

Then one day she called and said, "Guess what? I'm a foster parent to a puppy!" She sounded like her old joyful self.

"What does that mean?" I asked.

She explained that she met a woman who was part of a group that attempted to find new homes for dogs whose original owners couldn't keep them. One of the dogs was a boxer puppy who had been given to a shelter by its breeder because he couldn't sell it. The puppy had a deformed leg. "I'm just keeping her until they find a permanent home," Deborah said. "But she's adorable!" I sort of knew what was coming.

A month later Deborah adopted the puppy. "I couldn't give her up," she said. She named the dog Sweetpea. She was considering surgery for the dog's leg, but her veterinarian said it might not be necessary unless she was concerned about Sweetpea's looks.

"I love her looks!" Deborah told me. "She's the most beautiful thing in the world."

When I saw her with Sweetpea, I agreed. They were perfect for each other: the dog who needed love, and the woman who had so much to give. And I don't think it was a coincidence that brought them together. I think God had something to do with it.

—Phyllis Hobe

*S*EVERAL YEARS AGO our daughter Meghan, very distressed, phoned us to say she had lost Woo, her gray chow puppy, en route from Albuquerque, New Mexico, to our cabin in southern Colorado. When I drove up to the cabin the next day, I hung "lost dog" posters in restaurants, stores and gas stations along the way. Two weeks later, back in Albuquerque, Meghan got a long-distance call from a couple saying they had found Woo, matted, starving and footsore, resolutely headed down the road toward home. She had walked more than seventy miles from the place where Meghan had lost her.

The couple had seen Woo beside the road and recognized her from the description they had read on a poster in a restaurant earlier that day. They picked up Woo and took her to a motel in a nearby town, interrupting their cross-country trip to do so. They got the restaurant's number from directory assistance and called to ask for Meghan's phone number off the poster. They gave Woo water and dog food, which they bought at a nearby store, and petted her while waiting for her to be reclaimed, sacrificing a day of their journey.

Talk about Good Samaritans! Their unselfishness has become the measuring stick for me when I'm tempted to pass by someone in need because I don't want to interrupt my busy schedule. And if I start to forget, there's always Woo, now grown into a big gentle bear, to remind me.

—Madge Harrah

*V*ALENTINE'S DAY! For two days a beautiful box covered in pink-and-white crepe paper with two big red hearts glued to its sides had sat on the desk of our second-grade teacher. She said we were to bring valentines addressed to class members and drop them in the box. Then on Valentine's Day, we would have a party with pink lemonade and cookies and distribute the pretty cards. The whole class was excited about it.

A few days before the big event, Mother took me to the drugstore to buy my valentines. "I'll only need about six," I told her.

"So few? How many children are in your class?"

"I don't know," I shrugged. "I'm only giving to my friends, so six will be enough."

"You'll put a valentine in the box for every child in the class," Mother said sternly. "I'll call your teacher and get all of the names."

"I can't write all of those names," I whined.

"I can," she replied. And she did—she addressed a card for each child in the second grade.

The wonderful day arrived, and the boys and girls went up to the front as their names were called to receive their cards. The very popular ones went time and again. But I remember one little girl, the very shy one, who received only *one* card.

—Drue Duke

WHY IS ALL THIS FOOD being thrown away?"

Stan Curtis, a Louisville resident, was on the phone with the manager of a large hotel. "I've seen huge amounts of food being thrown into the dumpsters out back. Why?"

"These are leftovers from a banquet," the manager told him. "Company policy is to throw them out."

"I'm concerned about the homeless and hungry," Stan explained. "Would it be possible for you to call me when you have leftovers like that?"

The manager agreed, and from then on Stan made frequent pickups, delivering the food to area soup kitchens. Out of his vision and effort grew the nonprofit organization Kentucky Harvest, which now uses more than eight hundred volunteers to deliver food to sixty shelters and missions in Louisville and southern Indiana. This led to U.S.A. Harvest, which serves leftovers in more than sixty cities across the country.

What a powerful impact this one man's vision has had! It impressed me so much that now, in our house, I'm trying to make sure things we don't need aren't just thrown away, too. Just last week, our church asked people to bring clothing for the Career Shop (which outfits low-income people for the workforce). So I gathered up some of mine and Ken's nicer hand-me-downs and took them over there.

I also took grocery store receipts I'd saved in a program to help the nearby elementary school get computers, and egg cartons and coffee cans for their crafts activities. From now on, as I notice the unused stuff in my life, no matter how small or insignificant, I will ask myself, "Where can this fill a need?"

—Barbara Chafin

CHAPTER 4

Hints
of
Guidance

❧

He leadeth me in the paths of righteousness

for his name's sake.

—Psalm 23:3

I WAS WALKING TO MY CAR in the parking lot of our local hardware store when my bad leg (I'd had polio years before) buckled under me, and I fell, packages of potting soil and fertilizer spewing in all directions. An elderly man helped me to my feet and, after I'd assured him that I wasn't hurt, he helped me gather my scattered purchases and stow them in my car.

Of course I thanked him, but in the excitement I forgot to ask his name. I was so grateful for his kindness that I wanted to meet him again and thank him properly, so I placed an advertisement in the local newspaper: "Will the gentleman who helped a lame man in the parking lot of the hardware store please phone this number?"

It was a month before he called. He had been away on family business, he told me, and it was pure luck that a friend to whom he'd mentioned the incident had saved my ad to show him. He stopped me as I started to thank him again. "There's no need to thank me," he said. "I was only doing what my employer would have wanted me to do."

"Who is your *employer?*" I asked.

"God," he answered. "Isn't He yours, too?"

Well, I'd never thought of it that way. But it's true for all of us, isn't it? No matter who signs our salary checks, we're all working for God, not from nine to five, but twenty-four hours a day. That means we're on call to "do good unto others"—all the time.

It's something we don't have to think twice about. And isn't that a nice way to make a living?

—Walter Harter

*N*OAH IS SIX HUNDRED YEARS OLD *when God looks upon the earth and sees that it is corrupt. "I will destroy man whom I have created," says God. "I will bring a flood of waters upon the earth. Everything will die."*

But Noah is a good man who is faithful to his Creator, so God decides to spare him, giving him specific instructions for building an ark. He orders Noah to be sure that two of every kind of animal and bird and creeping thing of the earth are put aboard the ark, along with Noah's family.

Noah hears . . . and he obeys.

It happened a long time ago, but I remember it as if it were yesterday because it was an experience with God's guidance. . . .

I was visiting friends who operate a Montana cattle ranch—a "little spread" of four thousand acres. Although unfamiliar with ranch life, I accepted my friend Joan's invitation to ride with her out to a far pasture to check on a herd. Off we went, Joan on her black mare Midnight; I on a chestnut quarter horse Toby; and the old dog Buster at our heels.

When we reached the herd, Joan said, "There are too many cows grazing here; I'll take some of them to another pasture. You stay here and hold the rest."

"Wel-l-l," I gulped, "you know I've never done this. . . ."

"You'll do fine," Joan called out as she rounded up five or six cows and headed into the distance. Buster followed her.

So there I was, alone in the vast "Big Sky" country, responsible for a herd! It was scary. *What do I do if the whole herd takes off in different directions?* I worried. So I did what I've often done in unexpected situations, when in need of confidence: I sent up a prayer, asking God to help me.

Let the horse do it.

The horse? Puzzled but willing, I relaxed my grip on Toby's reins, slapped his flank and mumbled, "Okay, Toby, you're in charge here." With his years of herding experience, Toby knew exactly what to do. Back and forth we trotted, nudging a few cows here, galloping to head off a stray there. Soon I was having so much fun I forgot about being afraid.

Now, some people will say that the quarter horse would have acted instinctively even without my prayer. Perhaps. But the point is: I didn't know this. So for me it was truly an experience with guidance.

God spoke to Noah. Noah listened and obeyed. God speaks to us today. The question is: Have we listened? Have we obeyed?

—Eleanor Sass

*I*T WAS ONE OF THOSE DAYS: In the middle of rush-hour traffic there was road construction equipment ahead. In the distance I saw a beast-like machine laying steaming-hot macadam atop criss-crossed iron bars in the bedrock. As I glanced at the tightly packed cars around me, I sensed all the other drivers fuming and just as frustrated at the delay.

We finally approached the bottleneck as three lanes compressed into one. There, none of us could miss the huge sign that the burly, tar-spattered operator had attached on the machine's side:

The road to happiness is always under construction.

Our frustration dissolved into smiles, of course, and we waved friendly, appreciative acknowledgment as we passed.

It's sort of like the Christian life, isn't it? God's Word doesn't claim our path in life will always be smooth—because we all need repairs and construction along the way from time to time. But maybe our way will be smoother if we accept the rough spots for the small irritations they really are?

—Isabel Wolseley

ONE SUMMER WHEN I WAS A SMALL GIRL of eight or ten my family took a vacation on a quiet and beautiful Canadian lake. Our rustic cabin, set amid pine trees, was a short distance from the dock where a flat-bottomed boat was tied up. On our second morning there, my father, who loved fishing, announced that he'd go out before breakfast and try to catch a few fish. I'd never gone fishing before. The thought of catching fish and having Mother cook them for breakfast excited me. It was so different from our familiar routine at home. So I begged Daddy to take me along. He agreed, and off we went in the boat.

But our luck was not good. We sat out on the lake for a couple of hours without a nibble. Finally, Daddy said we'd better go back. As my father started to row toward the shore, I began to cry. I was bitterly disappointed that we wouldn't have any fish for breakfast.

"Stop your crying, Eleanor," Daddy said as he handed me his handkerchief. "Our not catching any fish today is a good lesson in learning how to take disappointments cheerfully. Life has a way of rewarding those who do, you know."

I wiped my eyes and blew my nose. Just then, a fifteen-inch northern pike jumped out of the lake and landed in the bottom of the boat where it flip-flopped wildly at my feet!

Now to you, dear reader, this probably sounds like an incredible fish story, but it did happen. And I like to think that it was the Good Lord Who arranged this minor miracle, just so that a little girl would remember her father's words always.

—Eleanor Sass

O<small>N THE FIRST DAY OF AUTUMN</small>, I walked beside a lake near Hendersonville, North Carolina, where I was on a retreat. There had been a lot of growth and inner changes in my life recently, and I was hoping to tap new courage to express them in front of others. You see, all my life I'd struggled with a need to please others, all the while putting aside my needs.

I sat on a splintered bench and gazed across the lake. Soon a small flotilla of ducks paddled into view, swimming across the water in chorus-line unison. When one duck turned, they all turned. When one quacked, they all quacked. They even speeded up and slowed down at the same time. As I watched them zigzag along predictably, I noticed one single duck swimming with the others, but clearly cutting her own path through the water. She sometimes turned left when they turned right, took little adventures on her own and quacked when the others were quiet.

I laughed out loud. God had sent me a duck, of all things, one that had a special quality all her own, and the courage to express it. She was clearly her own duck! And through her God seemed to urge me to be my own unique self, too. When I got up from the bench it was with fresh new courage (and a smile) in my heart.

—Sue Monk Kidd

*T*HE PARADE IS COMING DOWN THE STREET. The police escort has passed, motorcycle sirens whining. The flag has brought to attention the crowd lining both sides of Main Street, and here comes the high school band. How smart the members look in their blue and white uniforms! Every foot is in step, marching in time with the music they play.

And there is their director, Mr. Bennett, walking along beside the band. Strange. I have never really noticed him before, and yet I can't remember a parade when Mr. Bennett wasn't there. He just seemed a part of the background. Through the years, young musicians have marched and played and been applauded and gone on to bigger things. But Mr. Bennett has just stayed, growing older and walking quietly beside the band, keeping the members in step, ready with aid if any got too tired along the route. Just there to help, no praise, no glory for him.

My heart surges with thanksgiving for Mr. Bennett and for people like him, those faithfuls in the background, doing what needs to be done and letting others get the praise. I'm going to write some notes when I get home, and Mr. Bennett will get the first one. He will know that he is noticed and appreciated. And as the parade goes by, I'm making a mental note of others to whom I'll write.

Don't you have a list to start, too?

—Drue Duke

WHEN MY SON MICHAEL AND HIS BRIDE AMY returned home from their honeymoon, they stayed at our house before moving to the town where Michael would be working as the director of a high school band.

One night, Amy, who'd been giving Michael haircuts all through college, said, "Don't you need a haircut, honey?"

Michael, who was getting ready for two weeks of active duty with the Wisconsin National Guard, said, "I think I'll get a haircut at the barber tomorrow."

Trying to be the frugal wife, Amy said, "Michael, that's ten dollars! I'll do it."

We all went out onto the patio. Amy started clipping; Michael started grumbling. I was watching.

Michael began. "Put that other attachment on the clippers! You're going to make it too short."

"No, I'm not. This is the attachment I always use."

"No, it isn't. You're not going to get it right."

Oh, no, I thought, *their first marital fight.*

"You wouldn't talk to the barber like that. Why can't you be nice and just tell me how you want it?"

I'd be happy to tell the barber what I want, but you won't let me go."

At first, I wanted to side with Michael. *Maybe he should have gone to the barber. She's obviously not cutting it the way he likes.* Then I was on Amy's side. *She's trying so hard and she's doing a great job. Why can't he just appreciate her efforts?* But something, a guardian angel on my shoulder, perhaps, kept me from speaking any of those thoughts. Instead, I changed the subject to break the tension and before long, all three of us were chatting like old friends.

Before supper that night, Michael scooped his wife into his arms, apologized profusely and told her it was one of the best haircuts he'd ever had. He promised never to complain again when she got the clippers.

—Patricia Lorenz

"YOU'RE CRAZY STAYING IN NASHVILLE," my colleague was saying. "If I had an offer from a New York investment firm, I'd be gone like a shot from a gun."

Maybe I'm wrong to stay put, I thought to myself. *I like my clients, and I care about what happens to them. But I could really advance in the business if I went to Wall Street.* Then I remembered a sermon my dad had preached from the sixth chapter of Judges.

"Gideon faced a difficult decision," Dad had said, "so he asked God for a sign. Even today, there are times when God will make a path as clear as a flashing light, and other times when God doesn't mark one choice because many choices are acceptable. It's up to us to be faithful and invite God into our choices. Pray. And then listen."

So that's what I decided to do: Like Gideon, I asked God for a "fleece."

"God," I prayed, "I'm asking you to send me a sign. Send someone to guide me through this time of uncertainty."

Just two days later I received a phone call from John Beasley. John has worked on and off Wall Street in the investment business for more than twenty years. "I'll be in Nashville tomorrow," John said, "and I thought we might get together for lunch." The next day, I found myself sitting across a table from him. I voiced my concerns, and he responded with just the right questions. Seeing my work from his perspective, I realized how much I liked being exactly where I was.

You might call John's phone call a coincidence, but I don't think so. I believe his visit was God's answer to my "fleece." The truth is, I don't always know what's best for me, but God does. And if, as my dad says, I pray and then listen, God's answer will come.

—Brock Kidd

I USED TO FEEL GUILTY ABOUT THE BIBLES I'D BUY—and never use. Sometimes I'd buy them just because they were beautiful. There was one in particular—a purse-sized New Testament and Psalms. I loved it— the red pinseal Morocco binding, the gilt edges, the delicate odor of fine-quality paper. But the only time I touched it was when transferring it from one purse to another.

Until one day when I got stuck in an elevator in my office building. For a moment I was stunned. Then I started pushing all the buttons. Nothing happened.

It is hard to describe just how frightened I was—stuck all alone in a tiny cage with no way out. I sat down. I could hardly think. I opened my handbag, and there was the little Bible. I turned its pages to the fifth chapter of Matthew and gradually began to read. At first the words meant nothing, but, as I slowly read on, a whole world of comfort opened up to me. Jesus had come to earth to help those in trouble—He was with me now. I had to trust.

In ten minutes the building maintenance man brought the elevator up and released me, but in those ten minutes my little Bible was thoroughly broken in.

Now I know why I bought that little Bible. I needed it for just this occasion. Whether it is beautiful or just plain shabby, whether it is on a coffee table or tucked away in my purse, I want to have God's word near—for use!

—Christine Conti

ONE OF MY FAVORITE PASTIMES when I'm driving around town is to read the message boards outside churches. I shuttle my kids to and from school to piano lessons, dancing and Little League, so I have some favorite signs along my routes that I always watch for. Sometimes the message is welcoming: COME HOME. ALL IS FORGIVEN. Sometimes it's inspiring: THE WAY TO GET AHEAD IS TO GET STARTED. Often the message is humorous: WE ARE OPEN BETWEEN EASTER AND CHRISTMAS.

One afternoon, in the middle of a particularly rushed and stressful day, I passed one of the signs, and a question suddenly occurred to me: What does the sign outside *my* door say today? I remembered that morning. The sign my children saw might have read, SHE'S CRANKY TODAY, STEER CLEAR. Not a very welcoming message. To the other moms I hurriedly passed by at Maria's school in the afternoon the sign said, SORRY, TOO BUSY FOR YOU

TODAY. TRY AGAIN TOMORROW. There was no inspiration or laughter there either.

A church with signs like those wouldn't attract many members. Yet I'd never thought much about how my relationships with my family, friends and acquaintances are affected when the message I send out is less than welcoming and seriously lacking in joy. So I'm working on my personal message board every day now, and it's a challenge, especially on those less-than-great days. But at least I'm trying to post a message out front that says, YOU ARE WELCOME ANYTIME. I don't always succeed, but I'm sure it's an effort that pleases God. How do I know? Just the other day I drove by a church with this message: IF YOU'RE LOOKING FOR A SIGN FROM GOD, THIS IS IT!

—Gina Bridgeman

*M*Y FRIEND JOHN RECENTLY took his three-year-old son Joey to a Frontier Days parade. The street was crowded, but they found the perfect viewing spot—almost. "Their" corner was also occupied by a scruffy, bearded young man. So while Joey watched the procession of marching bands and prancing horses and floats, John watched the man. *Was he homeless? Would he ask for a handout or a place to stay?* John didn't relax until the man shouldered his way past them and melted into the crowd.

After the last cowboy rode into the sunset, Joey turned and asked, "Daddy, who was that man?"

John was about to say, "Oh, just some bum," when Joey added, softly, "Daddy, do you think that man was Jesus?"

"I'd always considered myself a mature, caring Christian," John told me later, "but Joey brought me face to face with a private sin: my judgmental attitude toward people who aren't like me. It's hard work, but I'm trying to follow Joey's example and look for Jesus in everyone I meet."

John's willingness to look for Jesus in other people may be the reason it's so easy to see Jesus in John. It *is* hard work, but I'm trying to follow John's example . . . and Joey's. Maybe someone will catch a glimpse of Jesus in me and continue the parade.

—Penney Schwab

*S*TEPH," I WROTE, "YOU ARE AN ANGEL in my path!"

"It's a lovely thing," she answered, "to think of oneself as an angel in someone else's life, though to me, an angel seems a being of light, something outside human boundaries. For sure, I don't feel like an angel of any kind right now."

My friend Stephanie and I have a lot in common, but our views on religion have been far apart throughout the years of our friendship. She was a devout Episcopalian as a teenager, but as a young adult became quite cynical about the church and all the hypocrites she saw sheltered in it. We became friends despite my Christian commitment.

But in recent years, a series of personal crises has driven Stephanie to look deeply for the meaning of her life. For at least ten years now she has been earnestly searching for truth. Her conversations and letters are a revelation to me. I marvel at her desire for spiritual enlightenment, and I am often reminded of Jesus' story of the man who sold all to buy the field where the treasure was hidden. Her periodic reports on her spiritual journey often surprise me.

"I focus on survival mostly," she wrote in the middle of multiple disasters. "I list over and over the cushions that have come with every blow to make the blow less awful than it might have been. I meditate and visualize God's hand under me—but I can't help remembering Job. Hanging in there didn't save him from the next blow."

I remembered that some years before I had told her that once when I was very ill I imagined myself in the hand of God. I could fall down. I could even hurt myself. But I could not fall off. And now I heard her wrestling with my childlike image with a maturity that put me to shame.

So when I said, "Steph, you are an angel in my path," I meant it literally. An angel is a messenger of God, and that is what Steph continues to be for me. Her probing questions make me think carefully before I give what may prove a too-facile answer. The integrity with which she searches makes me examine my own journey for living evidence of the faith that I proclaim.

—Katherine Paterson

I'VE HEARD IT SAID that when rodeo gets in a cowboy's bloodstream it never leaves. My youth was spent as a bucking horse rider. I traveled this world over until I quit the rodeos because Uncle Sam needed me in World War II. When I returned to the States after a long, bloody siege in Europe, I knew my days as a bronc rider were over. Adolf Hitler seemed to have taken my nerves.

But then I heard that the Wolf Point, Montana, rodeo paid big cash prizes. Though I was forty years old and scared, I decided to enter the bronc-riding contest. I rode a big Canadian bronc. But I had a terrible time with him. And as I held on to the bucking horse, I could see in my mind this pickup rider coming to get me. He wasn't dressed in cowboy garb. This fellow seemed to have a white sheet over him. His face I could not see. Over his shoulder he seemed to carry a scythe. I knew it was Death who wanted to take me off this bucking horse. In my mind, he sat me on the ground safe but I heard a message: *Don, you are bucking a young man's game. It's time you quit.*

Those words I still hear. They tell me there are some things we older folks shouldn't mess around with as we did when we were young. Sooner or later, there's a time when you've got to let go and say goodbye to out-grown things.

Is there an old habit, an outmoded dream, a stubborn attitude, belief or desire you're clinging to? Think a moment. Could this be *your* time to "cast away"?

—Don Bell

FOR DAYS I'D SUFFERED with what I call "a rushing spirit." No matter how fast I thought or hurried, a nasty inner voice insisted, *You're still behind.*

My list of things to do that spring Wednesday included going to our church at ten-thirty in the morning for one hour of solitary prayer. I entered the small, simple room in our church wishing I felt spiritual—like a real prayer warrior. I sat down in a metal folding chair and leaned hard against the heavy wooden table. "You know my heart and mind are rushed," I told God. "I don't even know how to slow down and try to hear You, but I desperately need to." I didn't really believe God would honor such a half-hearted prayer, but then thoughts began to glide into my troubled mind.

Remember the woman sitting alone on the bench outside the grocery store yesterday?

You slowed down because she was reading from a small New Testament. You saw her defeated face, and I even allowed you to peek into her lonely heart. You understood that she was hurting. You almost stopped, but then you hurried on with your groceries to the car. I had placed her there just for you.

"Oh, Lord, Lord! Forgive me. Yes, of course I remember. I saw her all the way home in my mind. I still see her! It wouldn't have taken long. I . . . I . . ."

She was My plan to help you slow down and learn to be still, child. I often reach you through unlikely people. Just sit here for a bit now while I comfort you.

—Marion Bond West

*T*HE FRENCH HAVE A PROVERB: *Si jeunesse savait, si viellesse pouvait*, which means, roughly, "If only youth had wisdom, if only age had strength." I thought of this one day last summer when I found my little boat swinging wide in deep water because the wind had changed and the tide had come in. "No problem," I said to myself, "I'll swim out, jump in, pull up the anchor and row to shore."

This was a maneuver I had not attempted for three or four decades. In the old days I would swim out, grasp the gunwale, give a quick heave with arms and shoulders, and land more or less gracefully in the boat.

So I swam out, grasped the side of the boat, and gave a confident little heave. Nothing happened. I gave a much larger heave. Still nothing. I seemed to be glued into the water, and a dark realization entered my mind. It wasn't Father Neptune who had me by the feet; it was Father Time. The lithe youth of half a century ago was gone, and here was this ancient character, thirty pounds heavier, in his place.

People were watching with amusement from the bank. Was I going to have to beat a humiliating retreat? Then the old French proverb came to mind. If age didn't have power, it was supposed to have wisdom. "Think!" I said sternly to myself. So I thought for a while. Finally I went around to the bow, grasped the anchor rope, tied a loop in it about the size of a stirrup, put my foot in the loop, and stepped grandly into the boat.

And the moral? Well, I guess it's that when the good Lord takes away one attribute, He supplies us with another. If we're wise enough to use it.

—Arthur Gordon

*H*OW OFTEN IT IS THAT I LEARN from those who are much younger than I!

I had been asked by seven young women, students at Baylor University and members of the church that I attend, if I would disciple them in Bible study. On this particular Tuesday afternoon we were talking about prayer, and I waxed forth (eloquently and informatively, I thought) on how we were to be specific in our prayers, spelling out to the Lord exactly what our needs were. I complained about those generic prayers like "Bless all the missionaries overseas" or "Watch over all the people who are traveling on the highways." "Even the Lord must find them innocuous," I said.

One of the girls interrupted me, "Oh, please, Mrs. Shellenberger, don't discourage anyone from praying those prayers. Usually, it is little children who are just beginning to pray in generalities. My parents are missionaries in Uganda, and they are in constant danger. I believe when some child prays for 'all the missionaries overseas' that the Lord knows the specific ones in need of special care at that moment and dispatches one of His angels to protect them from danger, or encourages them when they are discouraged, or strengthens them when they are weak."

Another young woman spoke up. "And who knows but that prayer for 'all the people traveling on the highway' may avoid a traffic accident because the Lord assigned that prayer to someone in danger at that very moment."

I still believe that the Lord wants us to be specific when we can. But to insist that this is the only way to pray is, I see now, to limit God in my mind and put Him in a box. Never again will I do that.

—Dorothy Shellenberger

*M*Y FRIEND BERNICE WAS DISTRAUGHT over her impending divorce. "There are times when I don't feel very lovable," she confided. "The thing is, sometimes I don't act very lovable."

I had no reply. Many times I, too, have needed to be loved, yet I've acted in ways that deserved just the opposite.

That afternoon, browsing in a local store, I saw a pair of white ceramic salt and pepper shakers shaped like kneeling angels holding lambs. I thought a gift might cheer Bernice up, so I hastily bought a pair without opening the box or undoing the bubble wrap the shakers were packed in.

The next morning, when I started to wrap the gift, something told me to take the angels out of their box and look at them. The pepper shaker came out first, just as I'd remembered it from the display—a sweet, tranquil lamb gently cradled in an angel's arm.

Then out came the salt shaker. Something wasn't right about it: There was a long, skinny tail hanging down over the angel's sleeve; the animal's face didn't look pointed enough and its ears were too upright and rounded. Then I looked at the animal's feet hanging over the angel's arm. They were definitely round-toed paws, not hooves! This angel was placidly and lovingly holding a lion cub.

I wrapped the gift and drove straight to Bernice's. When she opened the box, I said, "Look, Bernice. One of these angels is holding a lamb, the other is holding an unruly lion cub. Whether we're lions or lambs, the angels aren't afraid to hold us in their arms."

—Karen Barber

I'VE BEEN GUILTY IN THE PAST of envisioning all kinds of dark possibilities for my family and me, worries that greatly disturbed my peace of mind: What if our son were injured on his construction job? What if our daughter's car broke down in the middle of nowhere on her way back to college? *What if* . . .

Then one day I heard a story about St. Francis of Assisi that gave me pause. It seems that the saint was hoeing beans in a garden near the monastery when another monk rushed up and announced excitedly that the world would end in the next fifteen minutes.

"What are you going to do?" cried the monk.

"I'm going to finish hoeing these beans," replied St. Francis.

What a simple, commonsense way of dealing with unsubstantiated worries. Instead of distressing himself over something that might not come to pass, he put his faith in the Lord and got on with his everyday tasks.

I wonder—is there a lesson there for me?

—Madge Harrah

*S*EVERAL YEARS AGO, I did extensive research for a children's biography about Sojourner Truth, the remarkable black woman born in slavery who could neither read nor write. A devout Christian, she memorized the Bible and then devoted her life to walking the roads of America, preaching God's truth. When Sojourner reached her late seventies, Quaker friends in Battle Creek, Michigan, felt she was too old to walk and insisted that she use their horse and buggy. One day it occurred to them that Sojourner couldn't read road signs. "How do you find your way?" they asked her.

Sojourner replied, "When I come to a crossroad I let the reins go slack, close my eyes, and say, 'God, You drive.' And he always takes me to a place where I have a good meeting."

I felt that Sojourner was speaking directly to me. I'd always doubted my ability to make wise decisions. Often I'd spend sleepless nights mulling over problems and worrying over the choices I made.

Now, when I'm faced with a problem, I consider all possible solutions. Often I discuss the situation with my husband or a trusted friend. Then I visualize myself in Sojourner's buggy, let the reins fall loose, close my eyes, and say, "God, You drive." Within a few hours or days, when I'm thinking of something else, the solution pops into my mind. And, like Sojourner, I find that God always takes me to a place "where I have a good meeting."

—Aletha Jane Lindstrom

*I*T WAS MIDSUMMER and our family chugged down the highway heading home after a beach vacation. The needle on the gas gauge trembled on the red E and we pulled over at a service station. As the children poured out of the back seat, I headed for the water fountain. I returned to find six-year-old Bob stomping about in a mud puddle beside a leaky water spigot. His legs were splattered with mud and his white tennis shoes were unmentionable. "Bob!" I screamed, swooping down on him in fury, "get out of there!"

He tucked one black little shoe behind the other and froze. I dragged him out. "You know better than this!" I shouted. "Take those grimy shoes off!"

He retreated to the car, his eyes filling with tears. "I'll wash them," he said feebly.

"Off!" I demanded, glaring at him. I dropped the muddy things in the trunk and we piled back in, Bob's lip quivering and my anger seething.

We had traveled about twenty minutes when we came upon the most outlandish billboard on the side of the road. I read it, rubbed my eyes and read it again. Believe it or not, on it was a squishy black mud puddle full of little boys' feet and these immortal words, "Mud puddles are fun . . . a public service for little boys."

I peeped over the seat at the little wounded spirit in the back, my anger fading into remorse. The poor fellow had wandered into a mud puddle and I'd reacted as if he'd stepped into a smoldering volcano. *A "mud puddle event" and a "volcano reaction,"* I thought. There was a problem. I was sure I was getting a lesson from God that went like this: When annoying little frustrations and problems arise . . . pause. Don't lose perspective. Don't overreact. It's silly to treat a mud puddle like a volcano.

I leaned over the seat. "Hey, Bob, I'm sorry," I said. "Sometimes mothers forget that a mud puddle is just a mud puddle and mud puddles are fun."

He grinned back. "I know," he said.

—Sue Monk Kidd

QUESTION: How many psychiatrists does it take to change a lightbulb? Answer: Just one. But it's expensive, it takes a long time, and the lightbulb has to want to be changed.

Okay, so it wasn't a side-splitter of a joke, but maybe you smiled a little.

Laughter. It's like an emotional sneeze that clears the heart of serious sludge. Or a kind of temporary insanity that keeps us from permanent insanity. I'm no comedian, but making people laugh has been one of my most rewarding hobbies. Every day I post fresh cartoons on the bulletin board in my classroom. I sneak silly questions into the exams to lighten test anxiety. I tell my students about my most embarrassing moments. I play jokes on my wife and friends. This week I put a rubber spider in Sharon's saucepan. She got even with a plastic snake under my pillow.

I wonder what laughter could do for you? It might break the tension of a deadlocked meeting, or slow down an argument with your mate, or dissolve a painful memory of a big mistake.

"Some day you'll laugh about this," they say. So why not laugh now? Look for the funny side of everyday problems. Check out a joke book from the library. Buy yourself a toy and keep it on your desk. And while you are at it, keep in mind this thought: "Angels can fly," G. K. Chesterton wrote, "because they take themselves lightly."

Join the angels. Take yourself lightly.

—Daniel Schantz

CHAPTER 5

Beacons

of

Hope

Yea, though I walk through the valley of the shadow of death,

I will fear no evil: for thou art with me. . . .

—Psalm 23:4

WHEN MY MOTHER WAS A LITTLE GIRL, the family homestead burned down and almost everything they owned was lost. To this day she has a vivid memory of the family riding away from the gutted house in a horse-drawn wagon, her father, silent and inscrutable, sitting up front. The children looked to their mother to understand better how to deal with their loss.

My mother says she will never forget the expression on her mother's face. She was serene, smiling slightly and appeared totally unshaken. In one hand she held a single rose—the only thing she had been able to rescue.

As the children watched, she lifted the flower to inhale its lovely fragrance and then she allowed each child in turn to sniff at the delicate petals. No words were spoken. While the wagon carried the family away from their devastated home, the children and their mother focused their attention on the pristine beauty of a single red rose.

When as a child I heard that story, I thought my grandmother had made a poor selection as she ran out of the burning house. But now that I am a mother and grandmother myself, I am astonished by the wisdom and faith of this remarkable woman. Very simply, she gave her children the essence of faith: to let go and let God in, for if we are but quiet and listen, we will find Him speaking to us in even our most difficult moments.

—Marion Bond West

*J*ESUS HAS SPENT A FULL DAY *teaching along the shores of the Sea of Galilee. Now, at sunset, He suggests to His disciples that they take a fishing boat over to the other side. Halfway across, a storm arises. The disciples are afraid. They cannot understand why Jesus, Who is sleeping peacefully, isn't concerned. They stagger back through the wind-lashed rain and wake Him.*

Jesus sits up and looks around. "Why are you so afraid?" He asks. Then He rebukes the wind and tells the sea, "Peace, be still." After that comes a great calm.

Once I remember hearing those words, "Be still. . . ."

I was alone on the darkened beach when the heavy torrents of rain came. For the past twenty minutes I'd been stumbling up and down this remote Caribbean beach where I'd been vacationing, straining in the pitch black to locate the lights of the station house. Soon lightning cracked around me like a gigantic whip. Knowing it was dangerous to be on an open beach, I quickened my pace, tripping over a driftwood log. Panic seized me. In the blackness, all sense of direction was gone. *Oh, dear God, I'm lost! Please help me!*

I didn't really expect an answer, but all of a sudden it was as if something told me to stop. *Be still,* I seemed to hear. So I stopped, and at that moment a flash of lightning lit up the beach. Out of the corner of my eye I noticed a post I'd not seen before, with the numbers "7/8" scrawled on it. Then I remembered: It was a beach marker indicating seven-eighths of a mile. The station house was at the "5/8" marker.

Walk slowly. Watch carefully for two more markers.

A feeling of calm settled over me and within ten minutes I spotted the welcoming lights of the station.

As Jesus spoke to the wind and waves on that stormy evening hundreds of years ago, He still speaks today. Do you ever feel panicky, lost, alone, afraid? All you have to do is be still, very still, and ask, and listen. He will answer.

—Eleanor Sass

*T*HE CITY DUMP.

That's what it was that day in 1904 when a young black woman, Mary McCloud Bethune, saw it. Nevertheless, she and other willing hands built a shack on that desolate place, for she had a dream that, with God's help, she could help other black women learn to read and write. The first desks were wooden packing crates; the ink was blackberry juice.

As I wandered among the collection of tall buildings, classrooms and dormitories that is now Bethune-Cookman College, I stopped at a plain stone that marks the place where Mrs. Bethune's body was laid to rest at the age of seventy-nine. It had taken more than half a century for her dream to become a reality. The words carved on that stone told her whole story:

> SHE HAS GIVEN HER BEST SO THAT OTHERS
> MIGHT LIVE A MORE ABUNDANT LIFE.

She had not been alone in her long struggle. God had given her encouragement. She began and ended each day with prayer, asking His guidance. And He answered her.

God's help and inspiration are available to all of us. With His guidance men and women have produced electricity, flight, and the wonders of electronics, medicine and science. What marvels lie in your future? Seek His help in fulfilling your dreams; He will not fail you.

—Walter Harter

*F*OR WEEKS EVERYTHING had been going wrong. So much so that even my faith was slipping away, as though pulled by a great undertow. One morning I prayed to God, "You seem so remote. Please give me something to build my faith."

The phone rang and a woman said, "I feel so foolish for calling you. We don't know each other. But I read something you wrote in a magazine awhile ago. For two days the Lord has seemed to be telling me to call you to share a little incident with you."

Without pausing, she said, "I'm a nurse at DeKalb General Hospital. A while back a seventeen-year-old boy was nearly killed in a wreck. No one gave him any hope of living. We were to care for him while he died. He couldn't move, speak or communicate in any way. But God told me that he could live if only someone would believe and pray and not give up. I felt foolish believing when the doctors said he couldn't live. Nevertheless, I prayed and thought only about his being alive and healthy. Then one day, I said, 'Rodney, if you can hear me, wink one eye.'

"Very slowly and with difficulty he winked. Everyone on the floor went wild. My faith soared and I knew he would be healed. In a few months he was dismissed, alive and healthy."

The woman continued, "Does this mean anything to you?"

"Yes," I replied, aware of the tiny buds of faith that had burst forth in my heart. "The story is for me, to build my faith. Your miracle began with a simple wink. Mine can begin with something small, too. I can't thank you enough for calling."

There was excitement in her voice now. "I felt so foolish, but I finally told the Lord, foolish or not, I'm going to call this stranger."

—Marion Bond West

*T*HE FIFTEEN-YEAR-OLD GIRL with brassy hair, clouded eyes, and chipped vermilion-painted fingernails had been picked up as a vagrant. Now she stood before the juvenile-court judge and talked about angels. So, although Juvenile Hall was off my newspaper beat, I stopped to listen.

Sally had been the human target for a knife-throwing act in a traveling carnival until the troupe broke up, leaving her stranded. At fourteen she had run away from her stepfather's house, driven out by liquor, obscene language, physical violence.

No, she told the judge, she had no close relatives, but there was a place she might like to go. Once, when the knife-throwers were planning to go on a binge, they had dropped her off at the Sunshine Mission just off Skid Row.

"I spent several hours there at Christmastime," she said wistfully. "The nice lady let me help her. She let me be an angel in the pageant. I liked being an angel. And I liked the story about the Little Baby."

I visited Sally after she returned to the mission, where she was working as assistant to the "nice lady." She looked like a different girl—healthy, wholesome, and radiating happiness. "Now," she said simply, "I get to play a kind of angel all through the year."

—Elaine St. Johns

*I*WOKE UP IN THE MIDDLE OF THE NIGHT terribly afraid. It was pitch black in my room, and my brow was covered with cold sweat. I'd had a dream about going broke and winding up as an old man in shabby clothes on a tenement step, with no family or friends. The dream still seemed very real. I flipped on the light and glanced at the clock. It was 4:02 A.M.

Although we're not rich, we're certainly not bankrupt. Why, then, was I thinking, *There will soon be a total financial disaster!* If God was in my life, why was I fearful?

I thought about Jesus and His promises about fear. And in my half-asleep state, I began to dream about two little girls who reminded me of two of my daughters when they were little. The older one, Rachel, was consoling her three-year-old sister Janie, who had awakened scared and howling in the middle of the night after a Christmas play in which they both had been angels. In my dream, I heard Rachel say, "Janie, fear not! For I come to bring good tidings." And then she added, in a loud stage voice, "Jesus is right here in this room!"

"Oh," a tiny, tearful voice said, "okay," and Janie went back to sleep.

I smiled. What I needed there in the dark was not an answer to my financial problems but a Counselor, a Comforter to be with me through the long night. And, grateful that Jesus *was* right there in that room, I went back to sleep.

—Keith Miller

"Hi, Mom. I just thought I'd let you know that Cheryl's in labor." My son Paul sounded quite nonchalant on the phone, but after all, this would be their seventh child. I arrived at the hospital only five minutes after little Haley Sierra was born, and was greeted by my beaming firstborn son, who was now anything but nonchalant. "Just look at her, Mom—isn't she the most beautiful baby you ever saw? Perfect in every way!" She was. She really was. But, of course, I've felt that way about each one. The excitement and sense of wonder at the birth of a baby never diminishes. What a miracle a new life is!

In the twenty years I've been writing for the devotional book *Daily Guideposts*, I've shared the stories of the births of my eight grandchildren, each time finding some special meaning I thought you might apply to your own life. Every birth has had its own uniqueness. Yet a mysterious thread has been weaving in and out among the members of our extended family, a thread I've not told about before. It's this. It often happens that soon after the death of an elder family member, a new baby arrives. Grandmother Morgan died just before Karen was born; John was born shortly after my father died; Joshua, our first grandchild, arrived a few days after the death of my husband's father; Saralisa was born shortly after her paternal grandmother died; and little Haley's maternal grandfather died only a few days before she was born.

So what do I make of this? I don't think it's cause and effect. (Though at the time my father died, while I was pregnant with John, a friend consoled me by saying, "Your dad is with God, picking out just the right little angel to send into your family.") For me, the message has always been: *Every ending is also a beginning.* Whenever I find myself grieving a loss—a friend moving away, a cherished possession stolen, a death in the family—I see the faces of all those beautiful babies, and I give thanks for new beginnings, yet unseen, that are just a life-breath away.

—Marilyn Morgan Helleberg

EAK AND DEPRESSED from a monthlong bout with strep throat and respiratory flu, I struggled to prepare for Christmas. After the children and I baked cookies, my husband Alex took them up to bed. I longed to follow them and collapse in bed, but I sank into a chair and stared at the kitchen floor. *It must be swept,* I thought, *or flour, sugar and sprinkles will be tracked all over the house.* I begged God for the strength to finish this task.

When I walked outside to shake out the rug, I nearly gasped at the black sky sparkling with stars. Watching the dazzling sky, I thought of the shepherds, perhaps also out under such a sky tending their sheep. Little did they suspect that their sky—and their lives—would soon be ablaze with joy.

I wondered if I'd ever feel strong again. Yet my troubles seemed trivial compared to my friend Pat, awash with grief after two funerals this week for her dear brother and uncle. And my friend Rosemary, whose teenage daughter Ann ran away.

Looking up at the starry sky, I whispered a prayer for them . . . and sensed a message from the shepherds and angels: Be faithful to your daily work; persevere in prayer. The Messiah will come to you, to give you the help and strength you need.

Inside, I finished sweeping the floor, still coughing and needing my bed, but comforted . . . for my Savior was with me, in illness or weakness, in turmoil or grief.

—Mary Brown

"MAMA, CAN I HAVE A DOG? Just a little old dog."

I had abandoned the corporate rat race so that I could spend more time with my children. Now I could do all the things moms do when they are blessed with time to spend with their children. But I cringed when my son Chase asked for a dog. Our budget was tight, and dogs, I thought, cost money. "Well, just pray and ask God," I told him.

Chase prayed simply, "Dear God, please give me a little old dog. Amen."

The next morning, as we stood on the porch, we saw a little white and brown dog coming toward our trailer across the fallow field. It was an old, sway-backed beagle. Before I could say anything, Chase ran and wrapped his arms around the dog. "Scott!" Chase named him spontaneously. My son seemed very pleased to receive what he had asked for. But the dog was not at all what I expected.

Grateful for table scraps, Scott never wandered far from home. Old and wheezing, he ran just fast enough to keep up with Chase's four-year-old legs. As time passed, we all grew to love Scott. His big brown eyes said he loved us back.

—Sharon Foster

AITH...HOPE...CHARITY. The three "permanents" of our Christian walk. How often I pray for stronger faith! How frequently I need to ask God for more love! But until I begin to look for items to put into my spiritual Hope Chest, I never recall asking Him to increase my *hope*. . . .

My oversight seems all the stranger when I read what scientists are discovering today about the value of hope:

University of Kansas psychologist Charles Snyder tested thousands of college freshmen on a "hope scale" and found the level of hope a more accurate predictor of future grades than SAT scores.

Timothy Elliott, a psychologist at Virginia Commonwealth University, reports that spinal-injury patients with high hope have a far better recovery record than those with identical injuries and low hope.

And Dr. Aaron Beck of the University of Pennsylvania has developed a lack-of-hope scale to identify high-risk mental patients.

What is this all-powerful quality of hope? "Expectation of good" is the dictionary definition. But we can hope even without such expectations. Vaclav Havel, important Czechoslovakian leader, expected nothing good when he was imprisoned by his country's Communist regime. Yet he was able to write: "I carry hope in my heart. Hope is a feeling that life and work have meaning . . . whatever the state of the world around you."

The feeling that life has meaning . . . "Life without hope," Havel continued, "is an empty, boring and useless life . . . I am thankful to God for the gift of hope. It is as big a gift as life itself."

Hope as a gift of God . . . filling our lives with the assurance of His purpose in good times and in bad.

—Elizabeth Sherill

*T*HE FIFTEEN-ROOM VICTORIAN "dream" house we moved into quickly turned into a nightmare with the first heavy rain, which flooded the downstairs three times in six years. Insurance wouldn't cover the damage, we couldn't sell, and we used up all of our resources trying to hang on. We finally stopped fighting the inevitable, and the bank foreclosed. The week we received our notice to vacate, my husband Dennis lost his job.

One morning in my devotions, I was praying about the loss of our home. An image of our family living under a bridge somewhere filled me with panic. In the midst of my fear, God gave me a verse from Jeremiah promising "a future and a hope" (Jeremiah 29:11, TLB) and the image of His cupped hands holding a nest and in that nest our family. I realized that our security was in Him, not in a piece of real estate.

In the middle of our family trauma, I had a commitment to teach at a conference. The first night there I was wondering if I had made a mistake in coming. *Do I really have the strength to teach and give of myself?* But on my pillow was a small fruit basket and a notecard. On it was a drawing of God's cupped hands holding a home with the verse from Jeremiah underneath. I stood in stunned silence, holding tangible confirmation of God's graciousness and reassurance.

In your most dismal hour, believe that the Lord is with you . . . for He is. And keep looking ahead for God's promise of "a future and a hope."

—Bonnie Wheeler

P.S. By summer's end, we found a place to rent, Dennis started a new job and we received a large check from my friends at the conference who had taken up a donation for us.

CATHERINE AND JOE HAD BEEN MARRIED more than thirty years. They had no children and their lives were centered around each other. Then Joe died and Catherine was desolate.

"I can manage the day," she said. "I stay busy outside. But, oh, when I have to go in the house without him, the loneliness. . . ."

Last week in her garden as the day was ending, she looked toward the house with dread. "Lord God, have mercy on me," she whispered. "I am so alone."

At that moment, a large orange and black butterfly swooped past her face and perched lightly on her shoulder. It opened and closed its lovely wings as it rested quietly there.

"I stood very still," she told me. "I didn't want to frighten it. Then a strange thing happened: my own fear and dread seemed to drain out of me.

A great calmness came over me such as I hadn't known since Joe died. I took one step forward slowly, then another. The butterfly rode part way and then flew from my shoulder and landed on the screen door."

Her eyes, which had been sad for so long, began to twinkle. "I suddenly knew I was not alone. God is with me all the time, even in the house. I believe He sent His messenger, the butterfly, to remind me."

I still go to visit with Catherine each chance I get, but I've stopped worrying about her. She has learned the truth of His promise, "I will not leave you comfortless: I will come to you" (John 14:18).

—Drue Duke

WE WERE REMODELING a rental property in the country one summer when we discovered a mud dauber had plastered its nest on the newly painted weatherboarding under the back-porch roof. We certainly didn't want a wasp's nest on the porch so, using a broom handle, I poked the lump of mud until it crumbled down, and swept it away.

A couple of days later we returned to find an even larger nest in the same place. I knocked it down.

This went on for three weeks, with the nests larger, thicker, sometimes with tubelike openings to hold the larvae. Finally we found a nest as large as a boy's fist. No holes. The little tubes now held the larvae and all was sealed shut. The nest was finished.

I marveled at the determination of that mother dauber; to repeatedly mix mud just right; carry it, an unbelievably heavy load for her fragile body, in repeated trips to the rainproof shelter; secure it; then shape "beds" for her babies. The determination had to be instilled by God the Creator.

"I give up," I told the absent dauber. "Have your little daubers and be gone! Besides, I'm scratching all the paint off."

I've remembered that wasp's determination—her winning—in times that I've been tempted to give up. When a business failed; when rains washed crops out of our bottom field repeatedly; when I lost weight only to regain it; when a lawnmower wouldn't start; when youths we'd helped start a new life would backslide—until we reached out again. That little dauber taught us that all may appear lost, but you don't give up. You just build all over again because you were created in God's image and have within you what it takes to succeed.

—Zona B. Davis

*I*T HAD BEEN A DIFFICULT DAY at the pottery fair in Dresden, Germany. We had escaped the sudden downpour after closing by ducking into a nearby pizzeria. The rain pounded the streets at a nearly impossible angle, and the wind howled across the marketplace, funneled by the tall downtown buildings.

Our booths offered pottery from all over Saxony, and despite the dreary weather, the crowds had been good that day. Christival, a convention of thirty-three thousand young Christians from all over the world, had swollen the city to capacity, and between concerts and workshops, the enthusiastic participants had swarmed through the fair.

My friends Gabi, Conny, Hans and I had decided to attend the big Christival concert on the banks of the Elbe, and we were going back to the marketplace to pick up our jackets in case of more rain. But as we neared the market square, we stopped in our tracks. My jaw dropped, and Hans sank to his knees, moaning. Conny recovered first and braved what looked like a war zone. Our booths, shelves filled with the finest Bunzlauer ceramics, had been tossed across the square by the storm. Plates and teacups, jugs and vases lay crushed and scattered on the wet pavement.

Someone tapped my shoulder. I turned to see a group of four young people soaked to the skin. Their faces broke into instant smiles as one boy pointed and explained, "We saved some. . . ." Over by one of the market sheds, they had stacked crate upon crate of pottery. Out of the path of the whirlwind, more than half the booths' ceramics had been saved.

Hans stood and stumbled toward the stacked crates, staring in disbelief. Conny, Gabi and I descended on our sodden saviors with hugs of thanks. In the midst of the storm, God had been very active in the persons of four very wet, very kind, young Christians, who worked hard to save wares that weren't theirs, to help people they didn't even know.

—Kjerstin Easton

RIVING BY MY OLD GRAMMAR SCHOOL one windy summer day, my thoughts focused on my daughter Misty and her husband Indelethio. They were moving to New York City to pursue their dreams of dancing and acting professionally, and I was worried. They had no jobs waiting for them and had rented an apartment sight unseen. "Lord, give me peace about their decision," I prayed.

I noticed that the front doors of the school were open, so I pulled over and walked inside. The smell of chalk, paste and crayons reawakened pleasant childhood memories. I walked down the hall, listening to the wooden floors creak beneath me as they had some thirty-six years before. I opened the door to my first-grade classroom and walked in. Not much had changed: The desks were still in long rows, the group of tiny chairs still clustered in the back for reading time.

The one thing missing from the room was our wishing well. Our teacher Mrs. Brock had made one out of cardboard and painted it to look like gray stone. Often we were allowed to sit alone at the well and write a wish on a slip of paper. Mrs. Brock taught us that a wish is a tiny dream, and when you add a prayer, it gives your wish its wings to fly to heaven. I found a piece of paper and wrote my wish: *For my daughter and her husband to have a glorious life living out their dreams in New York City.* I added a prayer for their safety.

At that moment a gust of wind blew through the open windows. My slip of paper wafted through the air and floated out of the window. My tiny dream, on its wings of prayer, was on its way to heaven.

—Melody Bonnette

*M*Y MOTHER ADORED my little log cabin, and it was a special place of refuge for her when her cancer became terminal. When the hospital discharged her, Mother came to live her last days with me. Those rock-solid log walls became the backdrop for a hospital bed, suction machine and oxygen tanks, as friends gathered around with home-cooked meals and comforting words.

Some months before, I'd designed a sign and hung it in the front yard by the arbor. It featured an angel and the words, ON THE WAY TO SOME-WHERE ELSE, communicating the conviction Mother and I shared, that life is a journey where divine opportunities are often disguised as detours.

The afternoon of Mother's death, as the mortuary staff carried her tired and tattered earthly body through the screened-in porch she so loved, we children followed behind. When we came up the cobblestone path leading back to the house, I saw the words as if for the very first time: ON THE WAY TO SOMEWHERE ELSE.

With the Lord rebuilding my home and heart, my once-frightening detour had become the setting for Mother's ultimate journey: to her eternal home in the heavens not made with hands.

—Roberta Messner

*B*ACK IN THE NINETEENTH CENTURY, Robert Louis Stevenson, author of *Treasure Island*, suffered from ill health and couldn't live in England's damp, cool climate. So he and his family moved to a house on a hill in Samoa, a South Pacific island. Below, two villages of Samoans were at war. The problem was that the Samoans thought hurricanes were sent by angry gods who wanted a child sacrifice. Naturally, every time there was a hurricane, each village preferred to sacrifice a child from the *other* village, so they were always fighting.

When Stevenson saw this state of affairs, he worked tirelessly to teach the villagers that hurricanes weren't sent by angry gods, so that they would stop sacrificing children and warring with each other. Eventually, his efforts paid off, but in the meantime, his own health grew worse. It grew difficult for him to take the rough path down the hill. The leaders of the villages, now at peace, noticed this. And together they decided to build a road from their good friend's house down to their villages. They called it "The Road of the Loving Heart," a road they promised each other they'd never let grow muddy or lack repairs.

As the different villagers worked on the road, they were cool toward one another, only cooperating because they felt they were building the road for Stevenson. But as the work progressed, something happened. They began to know one another and to heal broken relationships, cementing the formal truce into deep peace as they worked together out of mutual love for someone. By the time they were done, "The Road of the Loving Heart" not only reached between Robert Louis Stevenson and the villagers, but among the villagers themselves, one that helped them live in peace and friendship always.

—Oscar Greene

*S*EVERAL YEARS AGO my family gathered around the television watching the saga of Humphrey the humpback whale. Remember Humphrey? He—actually a she—was the misguided whale who took a wrong turn and swam up a California river.

It was clear that if Humphrey didn't find her way back to the ocean she would die, and soon a bevy of workers were trying to turn the forty-five-ton whale around. They began tapping pipes beneath the water, trying to send her in the right direction. They continued until Humphrey turned and made her way downriver. When she finally broke into the bright, swirling waters of the Pacific, the workers cheered. Even in our South Carolina living room there were cheers. Humphrey was home!

I've never been physically lost like Humphrey, but there have been plenty of times when I've lost my sense of direction in life. I've taken wrong turns that carried me far from God and His plans for me. At times like that it's reassuring to know God always sends someone or something to find us and direct us back. There will be a friend who happens to say exactly the words you need to hear . . . a verse of Scripture dropped into your thoughts . . . a sudden insight from a book . . . even a casual comment by a stranger. All of these can be the "tappings beneath the water" that come to rescue us. For God has promised to leave the ninety-nine sheep and go after the one that is lost. He did it for Humphrey. He will do it for us.

—Sue Monk Kidd

WHEN TWO BLIND MEN ASKED JESUS to heal them, He first asked them a question: *"Do you believe I am able to do this?"* They answered, "Yes, Lord." "Then according to your faith be it done to you," Jesus said, spotlighting the role of faith as a precondition for their healing.

One July, my friend Betty was diagnosed with spreading breast and lung cancer and given little hope of survival, a few months at the most. I watched her go through normal phases of shock, anger and depression. Then one day she said to me, "In the deepest place of my heart, I believe I will get well. My God is vast and loving. And I have faith that there's nothing the two of us can't handle together! We're going to lick this. Just watch!"

I did. I watched her put her faith to work through prayer, healing meditations, diet, medical treatment, and a vibrant new attitude of hope and joy. She made time to laugh, sniff the flowers in her garden and listen deeply to her own needs. She left a job that had become stressful and deadening, and risked an exciting new career. She gave herself permission to try things she'd always wanted to do, from wearing purple to parasailing. She learned to paint, dance and celebrate her life. She reached out to others by forming a cancer support group and supporting others in their illness.

That diagnosis of cancer was six years ago. An inexplicable and spontaneous cure, the doctors say. But I've watched my friend and I'd rather believe that, just as Jesus told those two blind men, it was done to her through the mysteries and power of her faith. When God whispered to her, "Do you believe that I am able to do this?" she opened her heart and said, "Oh, yes! I believe!"

—Sue Monk Kidd

*I*N A CHURCH WHERE I ONCE BELONGED, there was a particular stained glass window that always drew my attention. It simply portrayed Christ standing with His hands held opened together in front of Him.

One Sunday I was sitting in church feeling the heaviness of a problem that had been troubling me for some time. My eyes were suddenly drawn to the stained glass window once more. The figure of Christ holding His hands cupped in front of Him seemed to be waiting for someone to drop something into them. I stared at the opened hands. *Give it to me*, the scene seemed to whisper. And in that moment I imagined myself reaching inside me and lifting a heavy stone of worry from within and placing it into the hands in the window—the waiting hands of Christ. And as I did, I felt a sudden lightness . . . the freedom that comes only from releasing our burdens and trusting them to God. The problem I had been carrying did not immediately resolve itself, but my heart was now freed to find a creative solution I had not seen before.

From that day forward, that window became my "worry window"— a place to which I could come and leave my fears and anxieties every week . . . a place that helped me learn to let go and trust.

Maybe there is an open pair of Hands waiting to receive your burden right now.

—Sue Monk Kidd

CHAPTER 6

Sheltering Arms

❧

Thy rod and thy staff they comfort me.

Thou preparest a table before me in the presence of mine enemies;

thou anointest my head with oil;

my cup runneth over.

—Psalm 23:4–5

*S*OME PEOPLE BELIEVE THAT MIRACLES only happened in Bible times, but they are mistaken. Miracles happen every day. I even talked to a couple of miracles once. They are David and Barbara Anderson, Christian musicians from Phoenix, who survived a 1993 plane crash in the Bering Sea.

On their way home from a trip to Russia where they had gone on a short mission assignment, their plane went down off the Alaskan coast. Amazingly, the Andersons and five others survived the ditching without serious injury. Amazingly, they escaped from the plane, which sank in seconds, hanging on to floating empty gas cans that had been loaded on their plane by chance. Amazingly, the pilot of another plane, running late, saw what he thought was a whale splash in the sea. When he heard of the crash, he remembered the splash, turned his plane around and "miraculously" located the surviving seven minuscule specks in the vast sea.

Amazingly, two helicopters were available and, amazingly, rescue workers were able to pluck the Andersons and their troupe out of the icy sea before hypothermia could claim their lives.

"We can't find enough superlatives to describe the work of our heroic rescuers!" Dave Anderson exclaimed. "Or thank God enough for sparing our group."

The experience gave new meaning to that old Cowper poem: "God moves in a mysterious way/His wonders to perform/He plants His footsteps in the sea/And rides upon the storm."

—Fred Bauer

*T*HE MORNING RUSH-HOUR TRAFFIC lined up behind me at the red signal. I stepped on the clutch to shift. The gears moved into neutral, then stuck. I knew the light would change any moment and the inevitable impatient honking would soon begin. I double clutched, praying, "Lord, please move this thing." Still the stubborn gearshift would not budge.

I felt angry tears stinging. "I'm going to be so embarrassed."

A glance in my rearview mirror showed cars lined up for two blocks. First in line, I saw the light in the opposite direction changing to amber, then green.

One last try. Nothing.

"Lord . . ."

Like a streak of lightning, a truck shot through the red light to my left, crossing the intersection just where my car would have been. I began to shake. It had been such a close thing. After a moment, I once again pushed the clutch. This time the gearshift went smoothly into place. I drove on through the intersection.

The gears worked perfectly at the next red light, and the next, all the twenty miles to work.

I'd been a half shift from certain death!

—Anna Mae Cheney

*I*N THE COLD PREDAWN DARKNESS our Japanese guide shook us awake. We were two American youngsters determined to climb to the summit of Fuji-san, the 12,300-foot sacred mountain of Japan. The evening before we had hiked up the steep, eight-mile trail in the moonlight, pausing for tea every mile or so at one of the rest stations provided along the way. At the highest rest station, not far below the peak, our guide had told us to sleep for a couple of hours before making the final ascent.

Now I was a bit tense, because a storm was coming, clouds had blotted out the moon, and we had neglected to bring flashlights. As we moved back onto the trail behind our guide, the wind hurled snow into our faces and the blackness was impenetrable. The path narrowed as we struggled upward and my sense of apprehension increased.

"Be careful," the guide warned as we reached the cone of the crater itself, "the trail here is only two feet wide."

I could feel the mountain like a wall on my left side, but on the right there was absolutely nothing, just utter darkness. I could not tell if the drop was ten feet, one hundred feet, or ten thousand feet out into that black nothingness. Suddenly my foot struck a stone and I stumbled and lost my balance. Terror seized me, but instantly, almost as if he had expected such a thing, the guide's firm, reassuring voice came out of the darkness: "Here I am. Take my hand. I know the way." His hand was there, exactly where mine was, waiting for me to grasp it. Which I did, and in a very short time we were standing on the summit of the great mountain.

That happened years ago, but I have never forgotten those words, because I truly believe God was speaking to me through the mouth of our Japanese guide. And all through the years since, whenever there have been troubles or difficulties, I have found reassurance in those quiet words: "Here I am. Take my hand. I know the way."

—Zacharias T. Bercovitz

_W_HEN I WAS A GIRL I had to cope with a trick knee. Five times my left kneecap had "jumped the track," and I had learned to pop it back into place myself.

But now I was no longer young. Lying on the cold black slab of the X-ray table, I was terrified. I had taken a bad fall, and, this time, I knew there would be no "popping back." It was a bad break. The grim face of the X-ray technician confirmed it.

As the ominous-looking X-ray machine descended over my knee, my fright increased. My pulse resounded in my ears as my heart raced—ka-boom, ka-boom, ka-boom. I gripped the edges of the metal table, fighting back pain and panic. And suddenly, incredibly, a message seemed to come to me, timed to the heavy rhythm of my heart: "Be still . . . and know . . . that I . . . am God."

In moments, thanks to those majestic words of reassurance, I had got hold of myself again.

That episode happened years ago. Now, whenever I feel overwhelmed, this little "heartbeat reminder" never fails to reassure me that God is with me and within me, always.

—Patti Phillips

TWO MEN WERE SENT TO A MOUNTAIN AREA to chart the territory for a map. They would go up on the mountain every day, and every evening they would return to their base camp. There they would sit around the camp fire talking with an old Basque sheepherder.

One evening the Basque shepherd said, "Tomorrow I must go with you on the mountain so you will not get lost."

The men said, "Why? We have gone up day after day. We know the way."

The sheepherder said quietly again, "But I must go with you." Again the two turned him down. The third time the sheepherder said, "I know the mountains like the back of my hand."

"We now have a map," the two men said.

"But there is no fog on your map," came the reply.

The two men went up the mountain alone the next day. And, true enough, a dense fog enveloped them. Soon they were lost. They floundered around for a long, long time. Just when they were ready to give up, the shepherd was beside them.

How often I think I can go my own way. Things go well and I believe that I have it made. Then something happens and I am lost. Yet, if I would look out, I would see the Shepherd beside me.

—Edward E. Lyons

ONE FREEZING NIGHT during the last week of basic training, my buddy Jack Daniels and I tried in vain to hammer our tent pegs into the crusty ground. The trouble was that we had been issued wooden pegs instead of the usual metal ones.

"Jack," I said, "it's going to be a long, cold night if we don't get this tent up." He nodded in agreement and we struggled on, managing only to break another wooden peg.

Then someone said over my shoulder, "You guys look like you could use a little help."

He was a tall man, a little older than Jack and me, and dressed in the same army-issue clothing. He had a small sledgehammer and six brand-new metal tent pegs. It took him no more than a minute to set up our tent. We stammered our thanks as he moved off to help another struggling pair.

"I was praying for help," Jack muttered, "but I never expected an angel."

I've thought about the incident many times since, and I now believe the tent-peg man *was* an angel. We never saw him again, and no one was ever able to account for his presence that night. Long after that army experience a situation arose wherein I was able to do someone an anonymous favor. It was a small thing, really, and accomplished easily, but I believe the deed was rather significant to the person it helped.

Why am I telling you all this? Well, just in case you have been a little skeptical about angels, I'm reminding you to stay alert. You might have been helped by one. And you might be called upon to be one.

—James McDermott

"Have I ever told you about the cupcake miracle?" my friend Gail asked me the other day. "It really was a sort of miracle," she went on. "I've always thought that if God spoke to anyone, it ought to be with thunder and lightning, but I guess I was wrong."

And she told how she had heard that a friend was celebrating her birthday one day. There was no time to visit her friend or mail her a card, so, half embarrassed by such a childlike gesture, Gail asked one of her children to put a pink candle on a grocery store cupcake and take it to her friend's home.

"I was sure she'd think I was crazy," Gail said, "but she called me the next day to say that she had been praying for a specific sign that God loved her. And when that silly little pink cupcake was delivered to her door, it seemed to her that it was a sign of God's love.

"So now I know," Gail said, "that God speaks to me in very small ways and sometimes with what seem to be just ordinary impulses. I've learned to listen," she concluded, "to God's voice in the ordinary."

—Lois T. Henderson

 Y FRIEND MARGE SHARED an experience with me just when I needed it. Some other friends had scoffed at my saying I sometimes felt led to make a telephone call, drop by a friend's house or write a letter. "Careful, June!" one of the group teased. "Remember what happened to Joan of Arc!"

But then Marge told me of her own experience. "I'd gotten up at six," she said, "so I could exercise on my stationary bike." She spends twenty minutes on the rig usually.

"I'd only pedaled for five minutes when I was sure I heard somebody call. A little irritated, I continued. Then, there it was again. And again."

Afraid something had happened to her husband or her mother, Marge stopped pedaling and called down the hall. Nobody answered. She checked their rooms. All was well.

"I felt strange then. Actually, embarrassed. I didn't even tell Mel or Mother, just started to get back on the bike. This time the voice was louder: 'Marjorie!' I hurried out into the kitchen and started the coffee. Again, 'Marjorie!'"

Alarmed by then, Marge picked up the telephone and dialed the number of her next-door neighbor. "I don't know why. Just because she was there, I guess." But there was no answer.

That, too, was strange. The ninety-one-year-old lady rises between four and five every morning. So Marge telephoned the lady's daughter. The daughter came, found her mother with a broken hip, called paramedics, and at last report, the lady was resting comfortably. "I'll always believe I served as a messenger for the Lord," Marge said.

Well, so will I. What's more, I refuse to be intimidated by well-meaning friends who choose to treat such feelings or voices lightly. Who is to say what God may whisper to me today? I will listen to Him!

—June Masters Bacher

*O*UR GOLDEN RETRIEVER ELMO has discovered a place of safety and comfort where harm cannot enter. Elmo's sanctuary is the back of my husband's white pickup truck. Whether we're driving to the post office or the city dump, or just out in the pasture to collect fallen limbs, Elmo can always find his spot and scrunch in.

When we are away on trips, we are told that Elmo climbs up in the truck that is parked in our driveway and snuggles right in. I've seen him just gaze at the truck with a look of pure love. Then for no apparent reason, he hops up into it, stretches out in the sun and falls asleep. The truck is Elmo's trusted friend; it never fails him.

When I couldn't sleep the other night, I heard Elmo barking from outside my bedroom window. A mental picture of him in his beloved truck filled my mind, crowding out my worried thoughts. Then I imagined myself jumping up into the arms of Jesus, like Elmo in his truck, experiencing His blessed peace. I held that picture in my mind until I fell peacefully asleep. In the morning, I was rested and ready to face a new day.

Today, snuggle into the waiting arms of Jesus, and find the strength and confidence to carry you through your day.

—Marion Bond West

I MUST CONFESS THAT I ALWAYS PRAY before I get on the freeway in San Francisco. I have the fanciful, but comforting image of me in my little blue car with half a dozen linebacker-sized angels (with full wing-spread, of course) riding guard.

The other day I passed a car stranded alongside the freeway. I prayed for the driver's safety as traffic whizzed by. Immediately, the image of one of my angels guarding the stranded motorist came to mind, and I was over-whelmed with the reality of the need for my prayers. Each time I pray for others, I am empowering angels to intervene.

Then the sobering thought struck me of all those times I neglected prayer: *Did that leave the angels powerless? The roadside driver unprotected?*

From here on in, I think I'll keep the angels on a full schedule. I don't think they'll mind.

—Bonnie Wheeler

IF YOU WERE FORTUNATE ENOUGH to have been a child during the late 1930s or early 1940s, then you may recall Saturday afternoons at the movies. In my hometown, there was always a double feature with cartoons, newsreel, coming attractions and a serial where each week the hero faced a life-or-death situation. One had to hurry back the next week to find out what happened! My friends Mary and Johnny and I would be first in line when the theater's doors opened at noon. Hours later, after having viewed everything at least twice, we'd emerge squinting our eyes in the blinding daylight.

What I also remember about those Saturdays was the tall woman whose job it was to monitor the children's section. She wore a white dress and carried a flashlight that she'd shine on any misbehaving child. We called her "Matron" because we didn't know her name, but she certainly knew our names. "Eleanor, your mother wants to have supper at six o'clock. You'd better go home now." "Mary, keep your sweater on. It's chilly in here and you were sick last week." "Johnny, sit down in your seat and be quiet."

Years later, I learned from my mother that Matron's name was Mrs. Bauer, that she was childless, and had taken the movie job not because she needed the money but because she loved children. And even though as a disciplinarian she might have been feared sometimes, we children loved her, too.

Matron made us feel safe and cared for. She, like our heavenly Father, was there in the dark, always watching over us.

—Eleanor Sass

I'D HAD A STRANGE WEEK. Monday, a crying little girl rang my doorbell. She had taken the wrong school bus and needed my help. When I drove her home, her mother said to me, "Robin's guardian angel must have sent her to your house." Tuesday, I found a gold watch on the floor of a theater where I had just seen a new play. When I turned it in, the usher said, "Somebody will be awfully glad you were here tonight." Wednesday, a woman called looking for my help concerning a court case on which I'd served as a juror several years before. "I looked through the phone book praying I'd find you," she said. And on Friday, a friend called me, frantic that she'd lost her purse. "Pray that I find it, Gina," she said, and I did. She found it the next day.

In each case the need was so obvious that I didn't have to think hard to know how to help. In a lighthearted way I pictured each of those people praying for help, and each day God looking down to see me once again in the perfect spot to be of some assistance. But it made me think: Are there times when God asks me to help someone and I don't hear the question?

I thought of a young boy I'd met at church the week before, whose negative attitude and rude language elicited a quick reprimand from me. I wonder if he really was asking for the attention that he's not getting anywhere else. Next time I'll try to respond more positively. What about my older friend who painfully recounted the difficulty of caring for her ill husband? Maybe I can offer her more than an understanding ear, even though she didn't ask for it.

Once I started listening for these "unasked questions," I began hearing them all around me. By taking the time to hear the cry in a child's voice, or really see the look on the face of a friend or stranger, I might discover a hidden need that God wants me to respond to, knowing that in that face-to-face moment, I'm the only one who can.

—Gina Bridgeman

NORMALLY, WHEN I GO TO NEW YORK CITY, I travel by bus or train, but on a recent trip I decided to drive. It was a poor decision. Since I moved out of the metropolitan area several years ago, I've lost the knack of driving in heavy traffic and avoiding pedestrians who leap out in front of cars to beat a changing light. Even worse, I stayed too long and found myself caught in rush-hour traffic on my way home.

I was inching my way along Ninth Avenue, heading for the Lincoln Tunnel, which would take me to the wide-open spaces of the New Jersey Turnpike, when the "Check Engine" light in my dashboard went on. Then the engine started making clanging noises. My car was breaking down—in the middle of New York City during the evening rush hour!

Gas stations are few and far between in a big city, and even though I was surrounded by cars, I felt utterly helpless and lost. Ordinarily, in that kind of situation I would pray—and I did—but, frankly, I wondered whether God could hear anybody calling for help in the middle of this crowded, noisy city.

Suddenly, there it was. On my side of the street, too: a little old gas station with one pump. A man was locking up the office as I pulled in and the engine died. He turned out to be a good mechanic, who not only replaced a broken fan belt but accepted this stranger's out-of-state check in payment.

Don't tell me God can't hear our prayers. He does—wherever we are!

—Phyllis Hobe

$\mathcal{M}$Y BACKPACK WAS HEAVY. Despite the fog and early morning chill, I was hot—and I still had another mile to walk to the Edinburgh train station. Suddenly, out of the fog, looking like he'd just stepped out of a Sir Walter Scott novel, a man approached. I grew apprehensive.

"Good morn'. Can I help ye out, ma'am?" he asked.

"No, thank you."

"I don't mind. Ye look a wee burdened."

"I'm certain, thank you!"

He shrugged. "I'll mosey on then."

The next morning, in a completely different part of town, I was holding a heavy bag and waiting for a city bus. Suddenly, out of the mist, the same stranger.

"'Ello, ma'am. Can I help ye today?"

I shook my head.

He leaned against the wall beside me. My apprehension increased. Not a single bus for half an hour! I prayed, *Now is a good time for a bus to come along, God!*

In answer to my prayer, my fear vanished, and though I'm not a person who hears God talk, I heard: *He's here to help you.*

The man stood by. We talked a little. Mostly it was quiet, an odd time of calm such as I've never experienced before, or since. Finally, "A bus be along the noon, ma'am," and he vanished into the fog.

I was not surprised when, less than a minute later, a bus wheezed out of the mist.

"No buses Sunday mornins, lass," the driver hollered. "I'm special run! But ye hop on! 'Tis not safe here!"

People to whom I tell the story often wonder if I'd met an angel. One thing I know, whoever he was, he was of God, sent to help and protect me.

—Brenda Wilbee

THE MONDAY BEFORE my son Michael's wedding, the reminder board in my front hall listed seventeen things that needed to be done that day to prepare for the rehearsal dinner for thirty at my house the following Friday and for the sixteen houseguests who would begin to arrive in three days. All I could do was shudder and ask God to send me a guardian angel to help me get everything done.

That morning, Wally and Shirley Winston pulled up in their RV. They were here to attend the wedding and spend a week in Wisconsin visiting old friends.

Shirley immediately saw the list on the board. "Well, let's get to work," she said. Wally gathered up brooms, the hose and my fifteen-year-old Andrew, and headed for the backyard patio to get it ready for the rehearsal dinner. Shirley and I headed for the grocery store. Then we started cooking. She not only thought up fabulous entertainment and food ideas, she also organized and set out everything while I was at the wedding rehearsal. She and Wally even stayed up late cleaning after the dinner party.

The dinner and the whole wedding week were a great success, but I could never have pulled it off alone. Through Shirley, Wally and my reminder board, God showed me how important it is to make your needs known to others—and that guardian angels don't always have wings.

—Patricia Lorenz

I RECENTLY WENT TO A RUMMAGE SALE held in a cavernous gymna-
sium in Las Lomas High School. I'll admit I was a bit startled when
the twentyish man behind me in line told his daughter, who appeared to
be about five, "You can go play in the toy section while Daddy looks at the
tools. I'll come and find you when I'm finished."

In this day and age? I thought. *After everything you read in the paper?* But the
girl nodded happily and skipped off without a backward glance. Still, I was
troubled. And although I wanted to say something, I didn't have the
courage to tell him he should keep an eye on his daughter.

But I decided that I would do just that, without saying a word. So
instead of looking for old books and bric-a-brac, I spent the next thirty
minutes watching from a distance as a five-year-old girl I'd never met
before nearly fell off an exercise machine, tried on a pair of shoes with

stiletto heels and a big purple flowered hat and then talked to her reflection in a big gilded mirror, and played with a set of checkers, another game and three toy trucks. Finally, when her dad—carrying a big box of nuts and bolts and a rusty lawn mower—came by to get her, I breathed a sigh of relief and got back to my junk hunting.

I had to smile to myself at how strange the whole experience had been. After all, though the two of them didn't know I was watching her, I *was* watching her. If she had gotten into trouble or fallen, I would have made sure she was all right. And then I thought, there is Someone Who is always watching me, whether I am aware of it or not.

—Linda Neukrug

I WAS TALKING TO MY POET FRIEND Paula about my apartment, which has been home for some twenty-three years. They have been, on the whole, good years in a place where I've always felt a sense of security.

"You probably have had a good angel looking after you," said Paula.

"Angels," I scoffed. "Don't talk to me about angels."

"You don't believe in them?"

"It's just that everybody is seeing them these days. It's like an epidemic. Okay, I know what the Bible says—they're real—but never having seen one myself, it's hard for me to believe in them."

"Oh," she said, "is it like your faith? You need evidence of something 'seen'?"

"Don't be smart," I said.

Not too long after that conversation, I had an appointment and crossed the street to my bus stop. As I stood there waiting, my eyes roamed over the facade of my apartment building. It's a large, prewar structure with some fanciful towers and a generous amount of ornate decoration. I found the windows of my apartment and the air conditioner for my bedroom and . . .

For the first time in twenty-three years, I noticed a head peering over the air conditioner, its wings looming neatly behind it, a figure carved in stone—an angel.

—Van Varner

"STOP, LADY—DON'T DO IT, you'll never make it!" The man screeched his camper onto the shoulder of the fast lane, perilously close to my car, jumped out and rushed toward me waving his arms.

It was my first flat tire. It caused my car to careen out of control on the freeway and had me so terrified that all I could do was pray a frantic "Help!" Fortunately it was mid-afternoon, before the crush of rush-hour traffic. I had waited for a long gap between oncoming cars and was just about to run across four lanes to the call box on the right shoulder when the man grabbed my arm and pulled me back.

"I'm pretty fast," I told him, "I think I can make it. I need to phone—"

"Listen, lady, on the freeway no one's ever fast enough to make it. A car close enough to see, and even a car not close enough to see, is a car close enough to hit you!"

"But what am I supposed to do?" I spluttered. "I have to get to a meeting."

"No meeting is worth your life. If you have a flat, or stall, and can't somehow bump your car over to the right lane, just stay in the car. Someone with a cell phone will call the highway patrol and get you help. You're lucky I came along. Here, I'll change your tire for you."

My eyes filled with tears of relief and gratitude. "Thank you, thank you so much." I paused, then smiled. "You know, your coming along wasn't just luck; I prayed for help."

He raised his eyebrows and grinned. Then, sweating with effort, he changed my tire. I handed him a twenty-dollar bill. "You saved my life. Please, the least I can do is buy you lunch."

He wiped his forehead with his shirt. "No way, lady. Just pass on a favor whenever you can. Help someone else in need."

—Fay Angus

HEN I WAS A CHILD, my world was a few miles wide—the distance to school, church and friends' homes. But it seemed enormous and sometimes scary. I walked to first grade with my friend Estella, who wore a St. Christopher's medal around her neck. He was the patron saint of travel, she explained to her Protestant friend as we waited for a green light at North Queen Street. "Every time I go out my door, I say a prayer," she said. "Our priest says God protects us in ways we'll never know."

"Well, we have angels," I said, quoting my Sunday school teacher. Together we made an ecumenical decision that God had us covered. When a car careened around a corner one day, missing us by inches, it confirmed our faith.

Then my world enlarged to high school and beyond. Though I still had a strong faith, my childish need for protection was lost in sophistication and self-confidence. I could cross the street—or the country—by myself. And I did—to Glacier National Park in Montana for a summer job with many other college students. The 1964 season opened with torrential rains and floods that shut us off from the outside world. At first it was a lark to us young people. Then the normally placid stream beside Lake MacDonald Lodge rose with terrifying suddenness to a raging river, crashing through the lodge's walls. Huddling in one end of the dining hall, we watched the water fold steel and wood as if they were paper.

Finally, we escaped to our dorm on high ground. Sitting on her bunk shaking and soaked, my new friend Joni opened her hand to show me a St. Christopher's medal. I closed trembling fingers around it, suddenly childishly aware again of how small I am, and how big God is—whether I'm crossing the street, the country or just stepping out of my door.

—Shari Smyth

IT WAS JUNE, and I was working as a wrangler for a rancher on the south fork of the Shoshone River near Cody, Wyoming. Each morning it was my job to wrangle in the saddle horses—that is, round them up—from wherever they had strayed during the night. I always kept a horse in the corral for this job, and one night I put in a green-broke colt. This was a mistake. A green-broke colt is a half-wild colt.

Before daylight I was up and saddled, and I heard the river roaring. The spring runoff had it full to the banks, a mad rush of driftwood and black water. As it grew light I used my binoculars to try to spot our horses. No horses. Finally I saw them out in the middle of the river on a sandbar island.

I knew they would never willingly leave the safety of that island, so I started out to get them. Pretty soon the rushing water was over my saddle.

When my colt got his nostrils full of water, he panicked and lunged out from under me. There I was, up to my chin in that icy water with trees and logs racing down on top of me. My horse and saddle were swept away; they drifted downstream until they came ashore. How I got there I'll never know, but I finally managed to make it to the bank. I sat there soaked and shivering, thanking God for my very life.

After I'd prayed, I looked toward my stranded horses on that island, and I could hardly believe what I saw. Those horses started into that raging river single file and all came safely ashore.

Those horses *had* been afraid of that river. Who started them off the island and brought them back home? I know Who. And I bowed my head and said another prayer.

Oh, I learned one other thing that day: save your best horse for wrangling when the Shoshone River is high.

—Don Bell

*N*IGHT FALLS AS MY HUSBAND DAVID drives down the narrow road that runs over the lake and through the pine woods to our family cabin in north Alabama. Sitting beside him, I look out the window into the darkness. "Better slow down," I say. "A little fox might dart out in front of the car."

"I don't think that will happen," David answers as he slows almost to a crawl. "The fox tends to be very—"

Before David's sentence is complete, a young fox leaps out of the dark brush and runs across our path, just inches from what would have been sure death a moment earlier.

"Wow! What a coincidence," David says. "I've never seen that happen before. If you hadn't said 'slow down' . . ."

"Funny," I answer, amazed, "I didn't even think before I spoke. What I said about the fox, it came into my mouth out of nowhere."

Later, David says, "All your life, you hear people say, 'trust your instincts.' Something told you to say 'slow down,' and you trusted it. I believe that's one way God is involved in our everyday lives. He speaks to our inner selves, and it's up to us to listen."

I smile at David. "God on a lonely road, looking out for one little fox. Imagine, God using my voice to keep His creature safe."

—Pam Kidd

*I*T WAS WITH A PARALYZING FEELING of fear that I lay in New York's Memorial Hospital that autumn day. My surgeon, probing the side of my neck, had told me that the melanoma, one of the deadliest forms of cancer, had returned. Even with radical surgery the prognosis was no better than three months to live.

The day before, Tib and I had gone to our church to ask our rector if he would pray for us. He took us into the sanctuary and while Tib and I knelt before the altar, Marc placed his hands on my head and prayed: "Extend Thy accustomed goodness to this Thy servant who is grieved with sickness . . . So restore him to his former health, that he may give thanks . . ."

Centuries-old prayers that seemed remote from my very present need. And yet, a curious thing happened. As our rector repeated the ancient words, a kind of heat flowed from his hands, settling in my neck. Marc looked at his palms in surprise and told us they were burning. None of us wanted to talk about it much.

And now here I was in the hospital. Alone. Scared.

Suddenly from down the hall came an eerie sound, warm and strangely touching. I got out of bed. In a nearby doorway stood a group of men dressed in long black frock coats and black hats. One of the men held to his lips what looked like an enormous animal horn.

"It's the Jewish New Year," another bathrobed patient explained to me. "That's a ram's horn he's blowing . . . a *shofar*."

Of course, *Rosh Hashanah*. This was the beginning of the year in Jewish tradition, a faith even older than our own, a faith that lifts human need to the same God. For me, and for the Jewish patient down the hall, the need was for healing. No wonder I felt less alone as I returned to my room.

It was the next day and I was groggily awake in the postoperative care room. My doctor was shaking his head in perplexity. "Remarkable," he said. Those lumps that had so alarmed him three days previously. All he had found in my neck were a few tiny dried-up nodules. . . .

Two encounters with ancient rites, both of them current in power and in hope. Today, years later, I'm in fine health, grateful not just for life but for the knowledge that nothing is really old—or new—in the Kingdom of Truth.

—John Sherrill

*S*CRATCH, SCRATCH. AT FIRST I THOUGHT the sounds were something wrong with the air conditioner just outside the window where I was working at the computer.

Scratch, scratch. No, the sounds were caused by something else. I opened the window and tried to see, but the air conditioner was too high. There was a cul-de-sac created by the overhang of a carved angel, part of the building's carved relief, and the sounds were coming from in there. I asked around, and finally the doorman said all-knowingly, "Swallows." Then he added, "Want to get rid of them?" He intimated he knew how.

"No," I said, and I meant it. I went back to work pleased that, although I couldn't see them, at least I knew they were there.

A few days later came a different sound: *Cheep, cheep.* Babies! I was triumphant! Now those country-lovers who decried my way of living, who were always telling me about nature in the raw, had nothing on me. In the middle of New York City I had provided these birds with an air conditioner for a home, and a fine one, as fine as that of the Psalmist who rang forth, "Yea, the sparrow hath found an house, and the swallow a nest for herself, where she may lay her young" (Psalm 84:3). Then it came to me how alike we really were. It was life, and I was part of it. It was transitory, for weren't we both on lease?

That was a long time ago. They have come every year, have had their offspring and then moved on, only to return. No, I don't know if they are the same swallows. After all, I've never seen them in their nest. Maybe, just maybe, that overhanging angel, that guardian angel, has been protecting us these many years.

—Van Varner

*I*T'S A VIVID IMAGE: the servitor's eyes fixed on the hand from which will come a signal. *Now! Act! Fill the role assigned you.*

Easy enough to detect a human master's hand-sign, but what about God's signals? Can we learn to wait for His silent *"Now"* in our hearts?

I know a man who did. I met Gregory Vojac at his home in St. Petersburg, Florida. But the test of his ability to wait had occurred in Atlanta, Georgia, during a catastrophic hotel fire. That night in 1946, Gregory awoke in his tenth-floor room at the Winecoff Hotel to the screams of fellow guests. The door to his room was hot to the touch. From his window all he could see was smoke—and an occasional plummeting form as people leapt from the floor above.

The only thing that kept Gregory from joining the 121 who died, he told me, was his long habit of listening to God's guidance—not only for His *what*, but for His *when*.

"Make a rope of bedsheets," he believed he heard God say, "and tie it to the center post of the window frame." Though he knew the makeshift rope would extend no more than two floors, Gregory obeyed. Through the smoke he heard the wail of sirens; he'd lower himself to the end of the sheets on the chance of being spotted by a firefighter.

Wait.

Wait? Wait while the paint blistered on his room door? But each time he hoisted himself to the windowsill, the order came again.

Wait. Not yet.

The floor beneath his feet was smoking when through the inferno of noise all around him came a quiet word.

Now.

Gregory lowered himself into the blackness outside. He reached the end of his sheet-rope, eight dizzy stories above the street. And just as he did, through the thick smoke directly below, rose the tip of a ladder, then the helmet of a firefighter climbing up.

—Elizabeth Sherrill

*H*AVE YOU EVER FELT GOD'S GUARDIAN ANGELS beside you in some time of panic or peril? I have and the peace that resulted is indescribable. Others who have experienced His protecting hand in such moments know what I'm talking about. One of those people is my mother.

After my dad's death from lung cancer at age fifty-two, Mother married a widower, a wonderful man, kind and loving. But one day her husband was stricken while shoveling snow from the front walk of their home. When she saw what had happened, she rushed to him where he had fallen unconscious. Mother ran back inside to call an ambulance, but, rattled and confused, she could not find the phone number. "Lord, help," she prayed. Suddenly, a woman appeared at her side and asked if she could help.

"Yes, please call an ambulance."

"I will," the woman said. "Go back to your husband."

The heart attack proved fatal, and in her grief Mother forgot about the stranger. Only later did she wonder about her identity. Had the woman been passing in a car and stopped when she saw the situation? Because Mother lives in a small town where people know almost everyone by their first names, strangers stand out—but none of the neighbors who came to Mother's assistance remembered seeing the samaritan described by Mother as young, fair complexioned, with short blond hair, a pleasant smile and a calm voice.

Some have suggested that she was only imagined. But Mother, a Sunday school teacher for over fifty years, knows better. The answer, she will tell you, is in her Bible—in Psalms, the ninety-first chapter, the eleventh verse. "For he shall give his angels charge over thee, to keep thee in all thy ways."

—Fred Bauer

*L*IKE ANY MOTHER, I had always worried about my daughter's safety. But after Amy Jo's divorce, I seemed to worry even more. How vulnerable she seemed—especially when she elected to take a class that meant she would have a late train ride home from Chicago two nights a week. I was especially worried about her getting safely to the train station. Her class was held in an area many blocks from the station, and I shivered to think of my petite, blond girl walking alone on the dark city streets.

I was driving home from Bible school on one of Amy Jo's class nights, trying not to think about all the things that could happen, when I seemed to hear a voice commanding: *Pray for a guardian angel!* I knew it was God encouraging me to trust Him, so I did. "Please, God, send a guardian angel to walk to the train station with Amy Jo tonight." I felt a deep peace as I turned into my driveway.

Next morning, I couldn't wait to talk to Amy Jo. "Any trouble getting to the train station?" were the first words out of my mouth when she came downstairs for breakfast.

She broke into a wide smile. "Nope! I had a guardian angel!" Amy Jo went on to describe how, on impulse, she'd paused at the door of the classroom and asked if anyone might be planning to catch a train.

"Yo, that would be me!" one of the biggest men in the class said. And he walked with Amy Jo all the way to the door of her train.

—Mary Lou Carney

ONE DAY BACK IN 1995, I told God that I didn't see how I could endure caring for another family member with cancer after my first husband Jerry had died of the disease in 1983. Now my mother's cancer had recurred after nearly ten years, and she'd come to live with my husband Gene and me. It wasn't just my fear of losing Mother, it was the battle I dreaded. Cancer just doesn't fight fair. I asked God for a word of encouragement. He often seems to speak to me when I run. As I turned the corner and headed down the road, a word popped into my mind and sat there as though it belonged: *Gone.*

"No, Lord. I hate that word. It's scary."

Gone.

"Lord, why are You giving me that unmerciful word. . . ."

Gone, Marion, as in "The cancer will be gone. All gone."

I stopped running, and still breathing hard, looked up into the cloudless sky for a sign, confirmation, some signal—anything to let me know that what I'd heard was from God. Cars zoomed by me, and all I saw was a dot of an airplane disappearing silently. Had it been my imagination? Was it wishful thinking?

Mother didn't progress with radiation as well as the doctor had hoped, and she flatly refused chemotherapy. Amazingly, a bone scan in 1997 showed a reduction of her disease. Her walking still wasn't very good, though, and I so dreaded the bone scan in 1998 that I didn't even call the doctor to ask about it; his nurse called me. "Hi, Marion," she said. "Your mother's bone scan shows no cancer."

"You mean no new cancer?"

"No. No cancer. We will need to treat the arthritis that's showed up, but the cancer appears to be . . . gone."

—Marion Bond West

CHAPTER 7

Glimpses
of
Heaven

∽

Surely goodness and mercy shall follow me all the days of my life:

and I will dwell in the house of the Lord for ever.

—Psalm 23:6

*I*N HEAVEN," SAYS MY FOUR-YEAR-OLD SON, with the confidence of a man talking about his native country, "everyone is one hundred inches tall." He goes on at some length about the geography and nature of heaven, what sort of boots people wear there (red ones), what the angels do all day long (play basketball), what's for breakfast (cookies).

These pronouncements draw guffaws and scorn from his brother and sister, but he holds forth with undiminished verve. "Yeah, I remember that heaven," he says, with affection. "God was there all the time. He really big guy. He laughing all the time. He funny guy. He have really big hands. He bigger than Daddy. I was not scared because He was laughing."

More scorn from his siblings and a grin from his mother, but his father is moved to ruminate on the topography of heaven, and not for the first time, either. Did not this boy come to me from God? Didn't his long-legged sister and his exuberant brother? And the lovely woman sipping coffee and smiling across the table? And the air we all breathe and the vast country outside and the crow on the fence cocking a curious eye at the heavenly boy in the house? None would be but for the Maker. And who is to say that this boy does not remember a place he was a mere four years ago?

So I listen with care, and hear of a country filled with joy and peace and light and laughter. Many days I think that I am in heaven right now, right here, in the sea of love that is my family. But listening to the little prophet at the head of the table, I dream for a moment of the world to come, the world we work for, in the end an ocean of love in which there are no islands of lovelessness.

—Brian Doyle

WE HAD GUESTS ONE NIGHT for dinner, and somehow we got into a discussion about heaven. One woman said, "I don't mean to sound blasphemous, but the thought of a heaven with gold streets and marble walls turns me off a little. I'd like there to be green grass, beautiful trees, lovely flowers, sparkling streams and the sound of birds singing."

"There will be—somewhere around," someone else said. "God would never take all those wonderful things from us."

Then I spoke up, "Well, I'm hoping to find a heavenly library there. I know I'll still want books."

"What would you like to have in heaven, Fred?" someone asked my husband.

"Two good legs," he answered, "so that I won't have to go around limping all the time. And the constant sight of God's face beaming at me." Fred had had polio when just a one-year-old baby, and one leg was so affected he had to limp his way through life.

Then a woman said, "We're individuals here on earth, and we don't all yearn for the same things. I think we'll still be individuals in heaven, and that God will give to each of us those special things we long for. Heaven is going to be all things to all people, and God is preparing it that way for us now."

I spoke up again. "I think one of the nicest things about it will be not having to pack anything up and move when it's time to go. I'd hate to think about getting in another U-Haul truck, even for a move to heaven."

Everyone laughed, but the conversation had touched all of us. The evening ended with the group holding hands and saying individual prayers. Each prayer carried thanks to God for our future heavenly home awaiting us.

—Dorothy Nicholas

*I*T'S BEEN THIRTEEN YEARS since I received that phone call from Mom, but every December I relive the shock. Her trembling voice sobbed, "Oh, Mary, Dad is dead." Snowmobiling with his friend in the wilderness of northern Montana, they broke through the ice and never made it out.

We buried Dad on Christmas Eve. That evening we wrapped a few last gifts, wondering how to get through the next day, the next year, without Dad.

Christmas morning we filed into church, our large family filling a pew. As the organist played the introduction to the first hymn, I squeezed my eyes tight, choking back tears. But then, somehow, it seemed as if God wrapped a warm blanket around my shoulders and whispered, *It's okay. Don't try to sing. Just listen.*

"O come, all ye faithful, joyful and triumphant." *But I feel sorrowful and crushed.* The voices swelled and rose with "O come, let us adore him, Christ the Lord," and inwardly I heard, *Come to Me in your sorrow. Come, draw near.* "Sing choirs of angels, Sing in exultation. Sing all ye citizens of heaven above." *Your father is now a citizen of heaven. As you worship Me, you are with him.*

As that realization dawned on me, an incredible joy welled up and I could join the singing. Worshiping Christ, Dad and I were together again. All of us singing in our church were united with those who had gone before us, adoring our Lord.

I would still have months of grieving ahead. Each December, especially, I miss Dad. But that joyful Christmas morning remains in my memory. And I can rest in its truth. Dad is home in his own country . . . heaven . . . a cause for celebration.

—Mary Brown

*M*OM, YOU'RE SUPPOSED TO DO 'Hawaii Five-Oh' when you turn fifty. It's a tradition. I'll pay your airfare," my oldest daughter Jeanne said.

And so we went, Jeanne, her boyfriend Canyon, my youngest son Andrew and me, on a dream vacation to Hawaii for fifteen glorious days. On the morning of day twelve we rented ocean kayaks, the only way to get to the most spectacular snorkeling spot on the Big Island. We kayaked a half-mile across the bay and spent the day smiling at a *gazillion* Technicolor fish underwater.

Around four P.M., we climbed into our kayaks for the return trip, the only living souls in that part of the Pacific Ocean. Exhausted, we lolly-gagged across the calm, crystal clear water.

Suddenly, huge fish were popping out of the water just ahead of us.

Dolphins! Dozens of them! We paddled like crazy to get closer, then sat silently when we reached the spot where they were playing.

I looked at Jeanne and Canyon in their kayak. They were speechless. As we sat motionless in that great ocean, the dolphins jumped out of the water, spun in the air and dove back in headfirst. They seemed as happy to see us as we were to see them, and for thirty minutes or so, we four were spellbound.

Finally, Canyon whispered, "This is unbelievable. It's definitely a 'God moment.'"

I nodded as six sleek dolphins, in perfect synchronization, glided within a few feet of the kayak Andrew and I were in, waggled their fins almost in a wave, then headed out to sea.

God had given us a preview of what eternity with Him in heaven is all about.

—Patricia Lorenz

*A*NYBODY WANT THIS?" My niece holds up Mother's church directory, a small paperback book with pictures of the congregation
and their addresses and phone numbers.

"Sure," I say, taking the book and leafing through it. How many of these
people I remember from my childhood! Thelma, who always played the
organ. Murl Weimer, a tiny, bent man with a huge heart. The Frame family. Nellie Fisher, who had been my kindergarten Sunday school teacher.
Suddenly, I notice several of the pictures have words scrawled across them
in pencil. The same words. I move toward the light so I can make them out.

Gone to heaven.

It's Mother's handwriting. I picture her here at the kitchen table—
perhaps she had just come from serving the funeral dinner for the family—
as she pens those three words. *Gone to heaven.* One more friend waiting
there.

I rummage through a drawer for a pencil and then find Mother's picture in the directory. How confident she was of where her loved ones were! And her confidence helps make me sure, too. *Gone to heaven*, I write across her picture, in a script not unlike Mother's own.

—Mary Lou Carney

H E WAS ONLY EIGHT YEARS OLD. For the past year he had been a cowboy and had slept every night with his stick horse Trigger. But now, after an August vacation with his parents in the Cayman Islands, he had a new ambition.

It was only the third day of school when he burst in the front door in tears. "Mama," Lowell wailed, "Carlos says he heard over the radio that we are all going to heaven on Friday! I don't want to go! I want to grow up and be a deep-sea diver." I sat in the wing chair in my daughter's den and wondered how she was going to handle this one.

She gathered her sobbing little boy in her arms and took him to the kitchen. I listened intently. She poured Lowell a glass of milk and gave him a gingersnap. "Lowell, honey," my daughter said softly, wiping away his tears, "I doubt that the man on the radio knows what he is talking about.

But someday, Lowell, you are going to go to heaven, and if it should be Friday, you won't be the least bit sorry because the deep-sea diving in heaven is something beyond anything you have ever imagined. You won't have to wear a snorkel or an Aqua-Lung or even a wet suit. If you decide to go diving in an ocean a million miles away, you can be there just like that." Sally snapped her fingers. "Besides, if you think the fish were colorful in the Cayman Islands, just wait till you see the fish in the oceans of heaven!"

When my daughter finally finished describing heaven, Lowell's tears had diminished to sniffles. "Well, all right, Mama," he wiped his sniffly nose. "I had better go call Carlos and tell him about heaven 'cause he doesn't want to go either."

How like Lowell and Carlos I am. Knowing what God has promised but still afraid of the unknown.

—Dorothy Shellenberger

I WAS STILL WAVING TO OUR DAUGHTER as she left for college after the holidays, when her little sister asked, "Why do people wave at people? Why do we wave when we say good-bye?"

And turning back with that sense of puzzled loss that so often follows when someone leaves, I, too, wondered: *Yes, why? Why do we teach even babies this first, and perhaps last, of life's gestures?*

"Wave at Daddy," we urge. "Blow him a kiss. Tell Daddy good-bye." And we are absurdly pleased when the little hand flies up in that spontaneous signal that announces long before words, "Look, look! I'm here!"

And all our lives, at parting, we are likewise impelled to hoist these mute flags after the futile farewells: "Do you have everything? We'll miss you. Give my love to everybody. Don't forget to write."

Now the dear figure that filled the house only moments ago is disappearing into a bus, or plane, or train, or car. Sometimes we glimpse a face at a window. And there's nothing left us but to stand waving, hoping until the very last second to be noticed, to communicate. It's as if these hands that so recently touched the child, the husband, the wife or the friend were striving yet to reach across the onrushing silence, the distance bearing down upon us, and signaling one more time: "Take care. I love you. I'll always be here. Come back as soon as you can. Good-bye!"

It always hurts to part from the ones we love, even for a little while. And we all dread the final parting. But, surely, the richest reward we have is Jesus' promise of eternal life. To know that for those who believe in Him and do our best to follow Him, there will be no final partings. We will be together forever in paradise.

—Marjorie Holmes

*E*VER SINCE MY GRADE-SCHOOL DAYS, I've loved to read about travel and learn about exotic places I longed one day to see: China's Great Wall, Egypt's pyramids, Norway's fjords, Greece's Parthenon or Mexico's Mayan ruins. But of all the wonders of the world, one place sticks out in my mind. How about this description?

- One enters this land not through a single wooden, iron or stone gate, but via any of twelve gates—each gate being "one pearl."
- The city streets are not macadam, concrete, brick or stone—but "of pure gold, like transparent glass."
- Those inside this land have "no more death, neither sorrow, nor crying," for "God shall wipe away all tears."
- There is no darkness—God's glory lightens this land.

In fact, turn to Revelation 21 and read about it yourself. No eye has seen, no ear has heard, nor can anyone even imagine such glories as are in this land. Better yet—being there is not for the few who can afford the trip or hold the winning ticket in a drawing.

This is the heavenly country, "which God hath prepared for them that love him" (1 Corinthians 2:9).

—Isabel Wolseley

$\mathcal{A}$S I HEADED UP THE DRIVEWAY for my morning walk, I was struck by how beautiful the world was. The air was crisp, leaves were turning, a few clouds sat quietly on the horizon. All was wondrous, but what took my breath away were thousands of jewels sparkling in the early morning sunlight.

I bent down and looked. Spiders had been at work spinning webs over tiny patches of lawn and each web had caught scores of dewdrops, which now acted as prisms breaking the sunlight into bursts of color. I couldn't wait to come back from my walk to show my wife Tib. But when I returned an hour later, the dewdrops had vanished.

Or had they? I knelt to look more closely and saw that the tiny droplets still clung to the webs, but the sun's rays no longer hit them at the right angle to create these flashes of color. The gems were there, but conditions were not right for me to see them.

The Bible speaks of angels surrounding us in their thousands. Yet only rarely have I met someone who has actually seen an angel. After that early morning experience with the jewels sparkling on our lawn, I understand a little better how this can be. Angelic hosts are indeed surrounding us always, even though the spiritual conditions are not right for us to see them.

—John Sherrill

*A*CROSS THE CROWDED HOTEL LOBBY, I saw the pastor of the church I had attended as a child. I had last seen him in 1969, when I was eight years old. But even though it was now three decades later and his face had been altered by the passage of time, he was unmistakable.

I knew he would need help to remember who I was, so I began to rehearse an introduction: *My name is Dave Franco. My mom and dad were part of your congregation at Alamitos Friends Church during the sixties. Their names are Ruben and Sally Franco. My sisters Laura and Karen were friends of your daughter's, and I knew your son Mickey.*

Feeling sufficiently prepared, I made my way across the lobby to say hello to my dear old pastor. As I approached him, his eyes caught mine, and before I could open my mouth, he said, "David! How wonderful to see you!"

Thirty years had passed. He had looked into thousands of different faces since then. I had changed from a boy to a man nearly forty years old. And still he knew me. What a welcoming feeling that was!

I think that's something like what it will be like when I get to heaven. The Lord knows me even better than I know myself, and when I finally approach Him, He'll give me the warmest welcome of my life.

—Dave Franco

*T*HE WALL CLOCK was ticking away my father's life.

I was a helpless twenty-one-year-old, sitting by the white-mounded bed that was slowly swallowing his great body into that sea, or heaven, where independent oil operators go when all the wells are dry and the last field pump has ceased. I could picture his heart as a rusty, creaking field pump, awkwardly dipping like an arthritic black iron woodpecker, sucking out the black gold from long-forgotten strata in the rocks.

And then the pump seemed to come alive, in a frenzy to get the last drop out of life. He groaned, and a hooded Sister of Charity appeared from nowhere and took his hamlike hand. "Can you hear me?" she said gently.

"*Umm.*" He nodded, his eyes still closed.

"Have you ever accepted Jesus as your Savior?"

He shook his head slightly.

"Would you like to?"

Silence.

As he decided, my mind flew back down the years to our childhood Depression dining table: Mother; my only brother, later killed in a wartime plane crash; and me, eyes wide as Father took us on imaginary flights to Paris, the Grand Canyon, Hollywood—places he'd take us really "when our ship comes in!" But the Depression had ground him down, and the ship of hope he'd seen so vividly had disappeared in a gray fog of unpayable bills and unspeakable fears.

"Do you accept Jesus as your Savior now?" the soft angel voice of the sister said.

"Oh, yes, I do!" he whispered, nodding, much to my surprise. Then he sat up in bed, wide-eyed with wonder.

"I see a ship!" he said.

And then he fell back and disappeared from my life and sailed into the "otherwhere" with Jesus.

—Keith Miller

*T*HERE WAS A TIME IN MY LIFE when my job was particularly stressful: I was going in early, working weekends and getting home late, unable to think of anything else but a TV dinner and the news and sleep.

Then one morning when the normal Los Angeles low clouds were absent and the sunshine was just beginning to reach the tops of the buildings, I was walking from the parking lot to my office when something made me look up. Against the clear, bottomless blue of the sky, three seagulls were wheeling and calling to one another, bright white against the background. Their motions were so lovely that my breath caught in my throat and I had to grab on to a parking meter to keep from falling down in dizziness.

Caught in the consciousness of beauty, I watched the three birds spiral and dart higher and higher until they were just specks. Then I let go of the parking meter and walked on to the office.

Somehow, that day, though the problems were the same, the stress was gone. I had been treated to a reminder of heaven that morning.

—Rhoda Blecker

AFTER MY MOTHER DIED, my siblings and I comforted one another sharing family memories. To my great surprise, I discovered that Mom had not told them about our sister Lois's near-death experience. So that year, in my Christmas card to my niece Judy, Lois' daughter, I included a note to tell her about it.

While in the hospital with pneumonia, Lois's heart had stopped. Doctors successfully stimulated it. When Lois opened her eyes she said, "I have seen God and He's promised I will no longer have to suffer from my illness." Lois had myesthenia gravis, a disease that had weakened her for years. Although her lungs continued to fill with fluid, she felt no need for the oxygen at her bedside. Exhilarated, Lois lived one more day. She couldn't stop talking about her visit with God. And then she peacefully slipped away.

As it turned out, Judy, too, had not heard this story. She still tells me, several years later, "Aunt Elsie, I keep your note in my Bible and read it often. It comforts me."

I can understand that comfort because I, too, receive reassurance every day from Lois's near-death encounter with God. On good days and bad days, I think we all need to be reminded that we have a brighter life awaiting us with God. Just as He promised.

—Elsie Larson

*N*OW THAT I LIVE ALONE, I find that decorating and maintaining even my small cottage can be frustrating and difficult. I miss the help my children used to give me whenever I was inspired to rearrange the furniture to make a room more comfortable. For instance, just this weekend I was standing in the middle of my living room—newspaper in one hand, coffee mug in the other—when I realized that I had no really comfortable place just to sit and read. So, with a sigh, I put the paper and coffee aside and pushed and shoved the sofa, the armchair. . . . Two hours later when I sat down to read the paper, I was exhausted.

I thought of John 14:2: *In my Father's house are many mansions: if it were not so, I would have told you. I go to prepare a place for you.* As I was ruefully considering whether I would be quite up to coping with a mansion throughout eternity, the second sentence grabbed me: *I go to prepare a place for you.*

I'd never really paid any attention to those words before. What a comforting promise. He's preparing a place specially for me!

So now I've been thinking: Even if my heaven is in a mansion, there'll probably be a cozy, well-placed chair, an ample end table and a very good light to read by. For He's prepared it for me. If it were not so, wouldn't He have told me?

—Marilyn Moore Jensen

*H*OLDING OUR NEW LITTLE GRANDSON, delighting in the wonder of tiny hands, button-nose and eyes blinking in the unaccustomed light of a bright new world, my heart skipped a beat as I thought, *If only my mother could have seen him.*

Just two years before, I had held Mother's frail body in my arms and whispered the gentle reassurance, "Don't be afraid, Mummy darling. You are going right from my arms into the arms of Jesus. He is waiting for you, and when you see Him, tell Him how much I love Him."

With a quiet little, "Oh!" as though surprised by some angelic light, she went limp in my arms and into the presence of her Lord.

Life taken. Now I was holding *life given.*

I was reminded of the story I'd heard of another new baby. "Come," said the young father, taking his four-year-old daughter by the hand and leading her to the nursery, where they had just tucked in her brand-new baby brother. "Come and say hello!"

The little girl pulled back. "I want to see him all by myself."

Both parents looked at each other, eyebrows raised. "You mean no one else in the room with you?" they asked with some concern.

She nodded, curls bouncing in agreement.

With some hesitation, they let her into the nursery alone, watching and listening carefully from around the corner of the doorway. Standing on tiptoe, leaning over the bassinet, she patted the baby: "Tell me . . . tell me quick," she whispered, "what does God look like? I've forgotten!"

—Fay Angus

MEMORIES ARE TRICKY THINGS. The other day, after all these years, I found myself remembering Aunt Jessie.

When I was a small boy growing up in Georgia, I used to play in one of Savannah's parks, where all sorts of people came to sit on the green benches and listen to the children skate past—*whirr, whirr* on the scarred concrete—and offer bread crumbs to the pigeons or peanuts to the sassy squirrels. I remember the wrinkled old fellow with the eye patch who sold peanuts for five cents a bag; we were sure he had been a pirate. And a young man named Beckwith, so crippled by polio that he had to lie strapped on a kind of wheeled stretcher; we were sorry for him. And then there was Aunt Jessie.

Aunt Jessie was a serene old lady in a neat brown dress who had occupied the same bench for so long that everyone considered it hers. We had been taught to be polite to our elders, so every now and then we'd call out, "How you doin' today, Aunt Jessie?"

Aunt Jessie would smile and say in her soft low-country voice, "Fine, fine. Just restin' here on His footstool, waitin' for my turn."

This answer always baffled us because we could see no footstool, only a green park bench. And we didn't know what turn she was waiting for. But last Sunday, when our minister read the passage "Heaven is my throne and the earth is my footstool" (Isaiah 66:1, RSV), suddenly I knew. Aunt Jessie was resting on God's footstool, the earth (Jesus Himself called it that), waiting for her turn to be called to join Him.

I used to wonder about Aunt Jessie, but now I think she had it all figured out. That was why she always seemed so peaceful. And that was why she smiled.

—Arthur Gordon

*I*N THE MID-SEVENTIES a dream came true, and I was selected to attend the Guideposts Writers Workshop in New York. Although I'd never flown before, I was feeling more excitement than fear as my husband Jerry drove me to the airport. But when my plane was announced, terror hit the pit of my stomach, and I whispered, "I don't think I want to go." Jerry managed to get me on the plane with the help of a smiling flight attendant. They pushed me down into my aisle seat and fastened my seat belt.

"First flight," Jerry told the serene woman sitting next to me. I glanced at her briefly. She was elderly, chipper, with fluffy white hair piled on her head, kindly eyes smiling from behind round glasses. In her lap was a well-worn Bible. She winked at Jerry, and he left me on the plane. I glued my eyes to the burgundy carpet, determined to stare at it all the way to New York—if we made it.

Trying desperately to help me, my seatmate asked lots of questions. When she found out that I wanted to learn to write, she asked, "What do you write about, dear?"

I swallowed hard, studying the swirling pattern on the carpet, and said, without looking up, "My faith."

When we were no longer on the ground, I started to hyperventilate. "Look, dear, please look," she said, taking my hand. "We are up in God's heavens. You don't want to miss this." I squinted until my eyes were almost shut and turned my head ever so slightly toward the window, fiercely holding on to my seat. Right outside our window, breathtaking clouds invited me to marvel. They were astonishing, miraculous. I opened my eyes and my mouth formed a perfect O as I leaned across the lap of my newfound friend. God's majesty once again proved greater than my old enemy—fear.

—Marion Bond West

WHEN MY WIFE PAM AND I drove into the parking lot, a mud-splattered, red pickup truck was in the space next to ours. The hood was raised, and the owner was leaning over the engine. "Car trouble?" I asked sympathetically.

He was a black-haired young farmer with sunburned forearms and astonishingly blue eyes. "Nope," he said, "it's time for Snowball's lunch, that's all." He pointed to a cardboard box at his feet and in it I saw a tiny white kitten, so young that its eyes were still closed. "We've had a long ride into town and I've had her milk on ice. I have to warm it up, so I put it on the hot engine manifold for a few minutes." He pointed and I saw a small nursing bottle, like a doll's toy, complete with nipple.

"Where did you find her?" I asked, faintly amazed.

"Didn't exactly find her," he said. "We have some stray cats around our barn, mostly pretty wild. This kitten's mother came right up and put her down by my feet. Then she ran away. I guess she thought I'd take care of her baby for her."

"White cats are sometimes deaf," Pam told him. "Perhaps this one's mother knew it was handicapped."

"Maybe so," the farmer said cheerfully. "But she'll be all right once we get her started."

We left him there with the kitten drinking thirstily. "That man is an angel," Pam said. "And the kitten's mother knew it."

"An angel with blue eyes and a red pickup truck?"

"It's not what angels look like," Pam said serenely. "It's what they do."

—Arthur Gordon

I'VE ALWAYS KNOWN that sooner or later I would have to come to terms with my own mortality. It's just that I would have preferred it to be later, rather than this much sooner. The doctor's voice was serious. "Get in here immediately. Your blood tests show an alarmingly low platelet count. We need to run more tests, and maybe even a bone marrow scan."

With the possibility of a terminal blood disease looming over me, the next few weeks were grim. That is, until the morning I was snuggled in my robe, nursing a cup of coffee in my favorite chair in the garden, and I suddenly found my gateway to heaven! It came early, as dawn pushed a crescent moon back into the sky and filtered soft light through a break in the bushes that separate our property from the large estate next door. It flickered shadows through a canopy of oaks and danced rainbows across the field of dew-drenched grass where deer come to graze. Caught up in the glory of the beckoning light, my heart followed it, up the river rocks that frame the curve of the driveway, beyond the screen of trees to the big house I knew was there but could not see. Around that bend, the light diffused, beyond the limits of my vision.

"Look, darling," I said as my husband came out to warm up my coffee, "there, through the bushes. That's my gateway to heaven!"

"What?" he mumbled, fiddling with his glasses.

"Sit down a moment with me. Listen. When the Lord takes me home, think of me walking through those bushes, across the grass, up the driveway and then to the house we know is there but cannot see."

He poured my coffee, then got up to go. He doesn't much like talk of heaven, this large, stoic, hard-on-the-outside-but-soft-as-mush-on-the-inside man. "No, stay. Listen. That's what you tell the grandkids, hear?" He said nothing. Then, as his eyes followed the rays of morning light, he silently nodded his head.

Thanks be to God, my sooner turned out to be later after all. My platelets were clumping, easily fixed. But someday, I know I'll be walking through my gateway to heaven and the beautiful house I cannot see but know is there.

—Fay Angus

I LAY ON MY LEFT SIDE, stretched out on the edge of the precipice. Desperately, my fingers clutched at the stems of the plants that were growing on the cliff. I have a fear of heights, and my head was spinning as I gazed down to the canyon floor. My shoulders and back felt like a mass of bruises.

A sharp impact spread pain through my right shoulder. No, no, I thought, *I can't stand another blow like that. I'll fall, I can't hold on any longer—*

I put out my hand to brace myself as I slowly opened my eyes and tried to turn over on my right side. I felt a little knee under my back and heard a sleepy squeal. *Mary again!* Our one-year-old was stretched out across the bed, her head resting on Julia's belly and her feet forcing me to the edge of the mattress. When she stirred in her sleep, she unleashed a flurry of kicks. *Amazing how powerful her legs are,* I thought.

I looked up at the clock: 6:30. *Maybe I can just lie here for another half-hour,* I thought. *I can't get up now.*

Another night of fitful sleep, punctuated by dreams of cliff edges and charging mountain goats. It seemed I'd always slept like this, dragged myself through a day of intermittent attentiveness at the office, ridden home on the subway in a semi-trance and faced another endless night. I hadn't had a full night's sleep since we all had the flu and slept in separate beds last fall.

I closed my eyes. When I opened them it was seven o'clock. I slid off the bed and went into the bathroom to take a shower. When I came out, Mary was up. She toddled over to me and grunted, lifting up her hands to tell me she wanted me to pick her up. When she was resting in the crook of my elbow, she put a hand on my shoulder and looked into my eyes. And smiled, and gave me a foretaste of heaven.

—Andrew Attaway

A Note from the Editors

THIS ORIGINAL GUIDEPOSTS BOOK was created by the Book and Inspirational Media Division of the company that publishes *Guideposts*, a monthly magazine filled with true stories of hope and inspiration.

Guideposts is available by subscription. All you have to do is write to Guideposts, 39 Seminary Hill Road, Carmel, New York 10512. When you subscribe, each month you can count on receiving exciting new evidence of God's presence, His guidance and His limitless love for all of us.

Guideposts Books are available on the World Wide Web at www.guidepostsbooks.com. Follow our popular book of devotionals, *Daily Guideposts*, and read excerpts from some of our best-selling books. You can also send prayer requests to our Monday morning Prayer Fellowship and read stories from recent issues of our magazines, *Guideposts*, *Angels on Earth*, and *Guideposts for Teens*.